THE

TELEPHONE

ANSWERING

SERVICE

INDUSTRY

PREPARING FOR THE FUTURE

PETER LYLE DEHAAN

The Telephone Answering Service Industry: Preparing for the Future

Copyright © 1998, 2023 by Peter Lyle DeHaan, PhD.

ISBN:
979-8-88809-060-2 (e-book)
979-8-88809-061-9 (paperback)

Published by Rock Rooster Books, Grand Rapids, Michigan

CONTENTS

ABSTRACT OF THESIS

THE TELEPHONE ANSWERING SERVICE INDUSTRY:

PREPARING FOR THE FUTURE

by

Peter L. DeHaan

Kennedy-Western University

THE PROBLEM

The telephone answering service industry is maturing and aging; it suffers from public misconceptions and image problems; and it faces pressures from competitive industries, increasing labor and technology costs, as well as a rapidly evolving telecommunications infrastructure. Many within the industry are concerned about what the future holds, wondering if and how they will be part of it. Around the country answering services are being put up for sale, while others are simply closing their doors.

Alternately, some telephone answering services are embarking on acquisition sprees and outsiders are entering the industry in increasing numbers. This contradictory trend only serves to heighten apprehension and make for more questions. What does this all mean?

1

How will the industry survive; how can it grow and flourish?

This document, and the research behind it, will attempt to answer these questions and make recommendations to survive and succeed.

METHOD

One aspect of planning is performing a SWOT analysis. SWOT is an acronym for Strengths Weaknesses, Opportunities, and Threats. A simple survey obtained input from those in the industry, compiling its strengths, weaknesses, opportunities, and threats. These results along with options uncovered in the literature search are combined to form a list of alternatives to be considered and analyzed.

FINDINGS

The final recommendations of the research are numerous, but unified. First a group of six core items, uncovered from the survey, form a baseline starting point. These six are: strive for flexibility, be customer focused, improve management skills, enhance service, enlighten staffing, and increase employment attractiveness. Next, are two recommendations to form the foundation for future planning; these being to perform a company SWOT analysis (as opposed to the industry SWOT mentioned above) and develop a strategic plan.

Three additional, nearly universal, recommendations are added to this foundation: increase rates, improve sales and marketing efforts, and capitalize on twenty-four-hour staffing.

Now, with these in place, the main recommendations can be brought forth. They are to diversify into telephone order-taking, pursue internet opportunities, and invest in technology. An optional parallel path is to pursue growth via acquisition.

These recommendations have been made to allow industry participants to prepare for the future. The final step is up to the reader to determine if the recommendations are applicable to one's specific circumstances and then to react accordingly.

THE TELEPHONE ANSWERING SERVICE INDUSTRY:

PREPARING FOR THE FUTURE

A Thesis

Presented to the

Faculty of the

School of Business Administration

Kennedy-Western University

In Partial Fulfillment

of the Requirements for the Degree of

Master of Science in

Business Administration

by

Peter L. DeHaan

Mattawan, Michigan

Chapter 1: The Telephone Answering Service Industry

Preparing for the Future

Introduction

The telephone answering service industry is maturing and aging; it suffers from public misconceptions and image problems; and it faces pressures from competitive industries, increasing labor and technology costs, as well as a rapidly evolving telecommunications infrastructure. Many within the industry are concerned about what the future holds, wondering if and how they will be part of it. Around the country answering services are being put up for sale, while others are simply closing their doors.

Alternately, some telephone answering services are embarking on acquisition sprees and outsiders are entering the industry in increasing numbers. This contradictory trend only serves to heighten apprehension and make for more questions. What does this all mean? How will the industry survive; how can it grow and flourish?

This document and the research behind it will attempt to answer these questions and suggest possible methodologies for survival and success.

Industry History

The telephone was invented in 1876 by Alexander Graham Bell, with the help of his assistant, Thomas A. Watson. This new device was quickly embraced by the business community but was much slower to gain acceptance as a residential necessity. Additional developments were soon to follow. In 1877 a basic switching device was constructed to connect five bank branches to an alarm monitoring company. The next decade saw the first long distance lines connecting New York City and Boston. By 1910 enough long-distance lines had been deployed to allow for the first transcontinental phone call to be placed (TAS History, 1989, p. 30).

In was shortly after this that various entrepreneurs spotted a need and began to explore the idea of a business which would answer telephones for doctors when they were out of the office and unavailable. In 1917, one such entrepreneur, Genevieve Kidd, who is generally recognized as the "mother" of telephone answering service, opened the first answering service. Called "Doctor's Exchange Service," Kidd opened her Portland business for "doctors, dentists, and professional nurses." Its sole purpose was to answer after-hours calls. Seven years later, in 1926, she expanded the concept to include local business and those wishing to expand into Portland by opening branch offices. Coincident to and independent from Kidd's efforts, Pearl Forester began a similar service in 1918 in Dallas Texas (TAS History, 1989, p. 30).

The year 1921 saw Physicians & Surgeons Exchange open in Philadelphia by Clark Boyton. Boyton is credited with conceiving the idea for the first switch board (a "stop" board, as it was then known). He convinced the local telephone company to build it for him at the then significant price of $4,600 (TAS History, 1989). This device was to serve as the model for telephone answering service equipment for the next 50 years.

In 1932 Richmond, Virginia saw its first answering service. It served 50 doctors at the astoundingly low rate of $2.50 a month. This year was also when Forester expanded her Dallas operation to include the business community when she added her first commercial account. The next ten years were a time when answering services began sprouting up all over the country. Although they were all independently owned and operated, they shared common methodologies and approaches (TAS History, 1989, p. 32).

The first services employed the elegantly simple technique referred to, "if no answer, call ..." (TAS History, 1989, p. 30). Doctors would tell their patients to, and footnote their advertisements with, instructions of a secondary number to call when their office phone number was not answered. This alternate number was in fact that of their answering service. Since all the service's clients used a common number for this purpose, those accustomed to dealing with the medical profession after business hours quickly learned the answering service's number, calling it regardless of which doctor they needed to reach. The answering service quickly and effectively became the focal point for all information about and communication with doctors outside of their regular office hours.

There were unfortunately two shortcomings with this approach. The first was that as the service grew it would become increasingly difficult and cumbersome to determine which doctor was being called, causing patients to be increasingly routed to the wrong practice. The other limitation was that patients would need to keep two numbers handy and know when to call each one.

To combat these limitations, innovative answering services began having the phone company install an "off-premise extension" of each doctor's line at the answering service. It was and is the same as an extension of the line in today's homes. When the number was called both phones ring; the call could be answered at either phone and someone at the other extension could even listen in (which was at times a source of frustration for both the answering service staff and the doctor). This was a step forward but required a separate phone for each client and each line. Soon services would grow to have hundreds of phones in their offices; they would sometimes use lights to show which phones were ringing. Sometimes astute staff would even learn the unique ring characteristics of a particular account and could tell which phone to answer just by how the ring sounded.

To deal with the problem of too many phones, the next iteration of the industry began using phones with multiple buttons, one for each line. Phones with 30 buttons were common, while some had as many as 100. Other services dealt with the multiple phone problem by installing a cord board, which was a modified telephone company PBX switchboard. A young entrepreneur, named Jay Freke-Hayes, who had grown tired of the multitude of phones, wires, and associated confusion, persuaded the phone company to make the requisite modifications and install the switchboard in his office (TAS History, 1989). Nicknamed the cord board, because of its numerous cords used to connect and answer calls, it handled up to 100 lines. Multiple cord boards could be interconnected to manage a greater number of lines. The cord board quickly became the mainstay of the industry and remained so for fifty years. Some services still use the venerable cord board to this day. In fact, all the above-mentioned methods still enjoy some, although limited, use.

The first innovation beyond the cord board was actually invented in the 1950s by William Curtin. Unfortunately, because of the monopoly status of the phone company (primarily AT&T) and the allied support of the FCC, Curtin had difficulty gaining the right to connect his devices to the telephone network. In 1968, the FCC's Carterfone decision stated that other devices could indeed be connected to the telephone network, if the devices were "privately beneficial, but not publicly harmful." (Newton, 1989, p. 109). This opened the door for Curtin and countless other entrepreneurs to design, manufacture, market, and install add-on devices connected to the telephone network.

Curtin's company, Amtelco, began manufacturing products in the 1970s to replace the cord board. These products offered new features and greater flexibility than the cord board and became the product of choice to replace the aging army of cord boards. Although other vendors were to join the fray, Amtelco's early entry into the market helped to establish it as the market leader. Amtelco's device, generically called a concentrator, took up to 100 off-premise extensions (lines) and "concentrated" them into a few lines (much like a funnel), allowing them to be answered on a basic telephone. Later, with the help of a basic computer display, which showed what to say when answering the line, Curtin's concentrator also counted the number of times the phone rang. In the event a call would ring too many times the equipment would automatically answer the line, playing a "please hold" recording for the caller. Many other vendors followed suit with concentrators of their own.

The next wave of innovation came with DID (Direct Inward Dial) service. Unlike a standard telephone line where there is a one-to-one matching of a number to a line, DID service matches many numbers to a few lines (which, in this case, are called trunks). It was realized that using the newly developed call-forwarding service from the phone company, each client could call-forward to their own assigned DID number. Whenever a particular DID number rang, it would be for a specific client. Again, Curtin capitalized on this new opportunity. He astutely developed an add-on device for the cord board. It would fit inside the cord board, allowing for DID service to be inexpensively integrated into the large number of cord boards still in service. He also upgraded his line concentrator to handle DID service, in addition to its original purpose of handling off-premise extensions.

In the 80s, DID service quickly became the mainstay of the telephone answering service industry, replacing off-premise extensions which were becoming increasingly more expensive to have the phone company install and maintain. Also, the 1980s witnessed the forced divestiture of AT&T and the birth of the personal computer. These two developments worked together to modernize and significantly advance the telephone answering service industry. Today, virtually all services over 100 accounts are computerized, answering calls by way of computer, typing messages into the computer, and using computer technology to dispatch messages to alphanumeric pagers, fax machines, and email addresses.

These computers instruct the answering service's employees, caller telephone service representatives (TSRs), how to answer the phone, what information to obtain from the caller, and how to process the information once it has been collected. The computer allows for speed dialing of pagers and other phone numbers and can remind TSRs to follow-up on pending messages. Since all the client information and messages are typed into a computer, it is readily available to any TSR, even those who may be working at a different location, who is connected to the same system.

The current phase of innovation employs an advanced version of caller ID, called ANI (automatic number identification) and the sophisticated PRI-ISDN (Primary Rate Interface Integrated Services Digital Network) service. In this scenario, the DID number has been eliminated and the clients all call forward to a common phone number. The ANI captures the called number (that is, the caller's number), the calling number (that is, the client's number), and the reason why the call is forwarded (the line is busy, wasn't answered, etc.) The called number is the key to identify which client was called, allowing the computer to display the correct account on the computer screen for the TSR. The calling number is automatically entered into the message form, while the reason for the forward is displayed for the TSR, allowing him or her to handle the call more intelligently, since they know why the call was forwarded to them.

Technical innovation is currently a driving force in the telephone answering service industry. Amtelco, along with Cad Com and Startel are the three major vendors providing equipment to the industry. Other vendors have smaller market share, pursued special niches, developed companion products, or made ancillary devices. Ironically, major telecommunication equipment manufacturers have occasionally attempted to sell to the telephone answering service industry but have been unsuccessful as the requirements of a TAS (Telephone Answering Service) are too specialized for their general-purpose equipment solutions.

Driving this current wave of equipment development is innovation from the telephone companies. As the monopoly status of the traditional telephone companies continues to erode, both from a legal and actual standpoint, they are increasingly forced to compete. This competition leads to new and innovative services, some of which are waiting to be harnessed by the telephone answering service industry. CAPs (Competitive Access Providers, which compete with the local entrenched phone company) and IXCs (Inter-eXchange Carriers, which compete with the established long-distance carriers) are leading the way with innovations as their smaller size and aggressive nature make them better poised to meet customer needs.

Table 19, in Appendix 1 summarizes this chronology of key developments in the Telephone Answering Service Industry.

Company Overview

The Company was founded in 1960. Like many in the industry at the time, it was started by a husband-and-wife team who split telephone answering duties into twelve hour shifts each day, seven days a week. For three years this pattern continued as they built their clientele to a point where they could hire their first employee. They started with a single cord board and added more as they grew.

Over the years they acquired other answering services in nearby markets. They also used DID service to expand into neighboring towns. They sold their interest to two of their former managers who have continued to grow and expand the business.

Today, the Company is comprised of seven offices, serving sixteen primary markets. Although their focus is a two state mid-western area, the Company can effectively serve all of North America.

Unlike many of its contemporaries, who have single-office operations, the Company's multiple offices have served to force it to develop standards and policies to ensure consistency among all offices and for all practices. These standards are in written form and are contained in a Manager's Handbook, which serves as a training tool for the new manager and a reference for the seasoned veteran.

The Company is privately held, and all financial information is proprietary. It is headed by a CEO with day-to-day responsibility in the hands of its President. Together the CEO and President oversee the four areas of the Company. These areas are Sales and Marketing, Accounting, Engineering, and Operations. Sales is managed by a Sales Manager, with sales representatives, called Communication

Consultants, operating from the various offices as dictated by market size. Accounting and Engineering are centralized functions, headed by the Controller and System Engineer, respectively.

Operations is by far the biggest portion of the Company, comprising over 90% of the employees, most as TSRs. TSRs work in all seven offices, though only four offices are staffed twenty-four hours a day. The seven offices are grouped by profit center, which is essentially a geographic division. Each profit center has one main telephone answering service system (also known as a switch) and the requisite ancillary equipment to support it. Two of the profit centers each comprise a single office, while the other two centers include multiple offices connected to centralized systems. The Company was a pioneer in this regard, being one of the first to connect two remotely located telephone answering services together, running on the same system, while retaining staff at both locations. This innovation allowed for increased economies of scale, reduced labor costs, and increased efficiency. Regardless of which office the call may come into, it can be answered by whoever is most available at any of the connected offices.

The Company is strong in its operations and technical prowess, but like many in the industry would like to do better in the sales and marketing area.

Over ninety percent of the Company's revenue is from traditional telephone answering service. About four percent is from voice mail sales and three percent from enhanced services. Enhanced services include telephone order taking, literature and catalog requests lines, dealer locator services, and phone reservation lines. Less than one percent of their revenue is from internet-related services. It is the expectation of management that most future growth will be in the areas of enhanced services and internet related services.

Purpose of Research

The Company is currently working on developing a five-year strategic plan. This is the first time long-term planning has been formally conducted by the Company. In past years planning efforts were generally done informally and only for the following year. While most of the strategic plan will similarly address this same one year time frame it is desirable to view it in the context of a larger interval and to see and plan continuity from year to year.

The purpose of this research, therefore, is to determine options for the Company's strategic plan, but not to determine the plan itself. Because many similarities exist between the Company and the industry as a whole, the author feels that the findings of this study are not only applicable to the Company specifically but will be generally relevant to the industry as a whole.

It is anticipated that several possible courses of action may be uncovered and suggested by this effort. It will be up to each industry member to appropriately apply these alternatives to their business, their goals, and their desired outcome. No one scenario is right for all answering services, therefore care must be given to correctly apply the findings of this research, which are generic in nature, to the specificities of the individual business environments to which it may be used.

Importance of Research

In informal discussions among telephone answering service industry participants, many consider it to be either a mature or declining industry. Among them, Mari Osmon (1996, p. 3) states candidly, "traditional TAS is on the decline." Oliver Shatz (1996, p. 12) adds, that "the number of telephone answering services has dropped dramatically over the past ten years." The perspective of the Company is consistent with these viewpoints.

Mature industries are those in which growth is slow or zero (Berkowitz et al., 1997, pp. 321–322). Any new sales or clients merely replace lost business, and those sales are typically made at the expense of a competitor. That is, as an industry, accounts tend to be traded between member companies as opposed to completely new accounts being sought and added to the industry.

A declining industry is one where revenue is decreasing and new customers and sales are not sufficient to replace lost business (Berkowitz, 1997, p. 322). Informal discussions among industry participants generally confirm zero or negative growth in the telephone answering service industry. The Company's experience affirms this view, although some offices of the Company have experienced growth which contradicts this perspective. However, the Company forecasts that such growth is not expected to be sustainable or long-term. Statistics confirm the impact these trends have had on the industry. According to the Association of Telemessaging Systems International (ATSI) there were 10,000 telephone answering services in 1988 (TAS history, 1989). Today ATSI puts the number at less than 5,000. This is a fifty percent decrease in nine years and should give pause to all in the industry to consider if they might be a causality of the next nine years.

Given the industry status as a mature or declining industry and the precipitous drop in the number of answering services, it is imperative for its members to carefully, thoughtfully, and pragmatically develop a strategy to deal with the very likely prospect of decreased service demand, decreased revenue, and shrinking profits. Failure of a company to devise and implement such a plan will likely doom it to failure and inevitable extinction. This is not, however, to imply that a plan, by its very nature, will ensure business success and continued existence. It is quite possible to plan for the future and still fail. Therefore, not only must a stratagem be fashioned, but it must also be both realistic and pragmatic. Then this blueprint must be steadfastly and successfully implemented, making midcourse corrections and adjustments as it unfolds. Lastly, only with some good fortune and favorable timing can a company expect their plans to succeed, allowing companies to survive in such industry conditions.

While future plans will, and should, vary from company to company, they will fall into broad categories of direction. These categories might include, leaving the industry altogether (that is, selling), diversifying into similar or unrelated business lines, focusing on developing and exploiting a niche market, consolidating the remaining market (through an acquisition strategy), or taking the company to another level (that is, launching a new business from the vantage of the current position in the industry). As previously mentioned, there will be no single suitable plan or direction which will apply to the industry as a whole; the desirability and correctness of each must be tempered with the personality of the company and its managers, the personal goals and time frames of the owners, and the specific business climate and financial condition in which the business finds itself.

Limitations of This Study

To expect that any examination will be perfect and without flaw or limitation is unrealistic and could cause those considering it to make incorrect or erred judgments and decisions. Because people are involved in any research effort, their biases, predispositions, experiences, and unique perspectives may skew, cloud, and otherwise impede the impartial gathering, analyzing, compiling, summarizing, and dissemination of information.

The author (who is also president of the Company under discussion) has been in the industry for over eighteen years and as such carries with him a perspective from inside the industry. If new paradigms are being sought, an industry insider might fail to consider them, discard them outright, or miss them completely. Also, the author's views and perspectives have been shaped by those around him, including the Company and industry for which the study is being conducted. This would suggest a tendency to confirm what is the current corporate view of the industry, be it correct or not. Also, the unique characteristics and conditions of the company in which the author works undoubtedly flavor the examination and influence conclusions.

Similarly, consider the circumstance and nature of those who wrote the articles and books which make of the literature review. What are their biases and attitudes? It is a given that leanings and predispositions exist, but one must consider if these are known or unknown to the authors and also if they are unrealized or intentional. Is there a hidden agenda? Does the originator have something to gain by expounding such a belief? Also, it is critical to consider the background of the authors. Are they from within the industry, in a related industry, or from a completely unrelated industry? Depending on the topic being expounded, the author's particular relation to the industry could be a benefit or a liability to their overall credibility and the specific relevance of their observations.

Lastly, consider the survey. A survey is limited in scope. It cannot address all issues from every possible angle; it is selective in what it asks for and, in order to achieve an acceptable response rate, it must be limited in length. The questions are, again, subject to the particular outlook of the survey's designer. Also, the questions can be interpreted differently by the audience than as was intended by the survey's creator. Likewise, the respondent's answers can be misunderstood by the author when the survey results are compiled and summarized. Naturally, the respondents carry with them the same biases and limited perspectives as mentioned above for the author of this document, the authors of other documents considered in the literature review, and the architect of the survey.

The characteristics of the target group will correspondingly impact any conclusions made based on survey answers. The size of the target group is a consideration. Is it sufficiently large enough to gain an acceptable response for the results to be significant? Also, what is the response rate of the survey? How was the audience targeted; how was the survey disseminated; and how were the responses gathered? The answers to each of these questions suggest the validity, relevance, and reliability of the raw results, as well as the conclusions derived from them. These issues will be addressed and explored in greater detail in chapter three.

Overview of the Study

The results of this study have important ramifications, not only for the Company, but for the industry as a whole. This study can provide significant input which will help companies to continue to exist and to enhance their future prospects. It is, however, important to interpret and apply the results of this study, and the corresponding literature search and survey, with an open, yet guarded, mind. Readers should take care to consider the limitations of the research before applying the principles and observations herein and to do so only after giving them careful consideration, ensuring that they are relevant to the specific situation to which they may be applied.

Chapter 2: Review of the Literature

Introduction

A literature search on the topic of "telephone answering service" yielded little information. No books could be found which have been written on the subject and articles written outside the industry are virtually nonexistent. What was found were articles from a limited number of industry sources and publications. These tended to represent the views of a limited number of movers and shakers within the industry. To supplement these sources, the search was expanded to the broader call center industry and telemarketing category. Beyond that is a vast collection of general business books and publications.

Insider Viewpoints

Many of the thousands of telephone answering services which operate in the United States today, do so in a virtual vacuum. They are unaware of the many various industry organizations and user groups; they are content to go it alone and to exist without the input, ideas, and opinions of others in the industry. Most of the larger and more successful operations, however, do make use of these industry associations and user groups. They join the groups, attending conventions, meetings, and seminars. They serve on boards and committees and make presentations; they give and they share, and they try to make the industry better for their effort. The largest and most ubiquitous such industry organization is ATSI, The Association of Telemessaging Services International. ATSI has an annual convention, which brings together the owner/manager and the vendor, along with speakers and presentations both from within and outside the industry. ATSI also publishes Answer magazine, the perennial publication of the industry. The annual convention and the Answer publication combine to offer an effective and concise view of the industry from within itself.

Tedd Smith, chair of the 1996 convention, wrote an article in Answer magazine entitled, "How to Surf a Billion Dollar Wave." He quoted from a study by ATSI which found that telemessaging services (that is, answering services) are expected to grow at 12 percent a year and surpass the $3 billion dollar mark by the year 2000. Smith acknowledged that "competition for [this $3 billion] will be fierce" (1996, p. 9). He continued to profoundly state that, "to capitalize on the opportunities that lie ahead, we must continually re-educate ourselves, reformulate our business strategies and goals and refocus our sights on the future—a time when telemessaging will be radically different from what we know today" (p. 9).

In the summer 1996 issue of Answer, ATSI president, Mark Hastings was interviewed. Although the interview focused mostly on the success of that year's conference, Hastings did make some remarks about the present condition of and future opportunities for the telephone answering service (TAS) industry. He stated that, "Most people have a fairly good perception of answering services" (Hastings, 1996, p. 12). However, he went on to admit that some have had bad experiences. He was concerned that there was a general perception among the public that answering services are little more than message takers. There are now more choices than ever in the area of communications. This includes voice mail, cellular phones, and advanced paging systems. However, this new technology does not detract from the telephone answering service industry, but rather it enhances it and allows for expansion into new markets that were never before accessible. Hastings foresaw future opportunities including order taking, order processing, and the internet. "We're at a crossroads in this industry as a whole," he stated. "It will continue to change in terms of the options available to traditional customers" (Hastings, 1996, p. 12).

Hastings also addressed the emergence and increasing prevalence of call centers. The divestiture of AT&T in 1984 and the subsequent explosion of 800 number usage paved the way for call centers to open, grow, and flourish. The ever-increasing power of computers and PCs, coupled with decreasing costs of technology and telephony usage have served to propel the call center industry to the place it is today (Hastings, 1996, pp. 12–13).

Hasting's predecessor as President of ATSI was Bud Taylor (1995) who pragmatically stated the obvious that, "it's very difficult to predict what the future holds for this industry." He went on, however, to prophetically add that "the possibilities will be truly limitless" (Taylor, 1995, pp. 16–17).

Another article about the state of the industry, which appeared in *Answer* magazine, included an interview with Peter DeHaan, the researcher and compiler of this information. Looking back, over the past ten years, the industry has witnessed an evolution resulting from two seemingly unrelated, but nonetheless simultaneous developments. The first was the forced divestiture of AT&T, which took years to completely unfold. While the second was the introduction of the personal computer and its long-ranging impact. To make a long history short, these two events resulted in two separate yet converging dichotomies. One being more telephony options at lower costs and the other, inexpensive yet powerful computers. These trends can be simply summarized as "more for less"—and they continue to exist today. Together they have conspired to make technology cheap, and options abound for the TAS industry and all business as a whole. They allowed and will continue to allow the industry to expand its offerings and reign in expenses. These trends should be expected to continue to occur (Kuhn, 1995, p. 15).

Add to this, the realization that the industry is classified as a mature industry. The characteristics of a mature industry include increasing competition for market share, downward pressure on price, and diminished profits. "To deal with this reality, we must formulate a transition plan." Telephone answering services should position themselves to acquire, be acquired, or find a market niche. Once accomplished, a bold move will be required to take the industry to the next level or "to create a whole new industry" (Kuhn, 1995, p. 15).

An industry leader and perennial favorite on the industry talk circuit is Mari Osmon. Her 1996 ATSI convention presentation and companion follow-up article in *Answer* magazine was entitled "From TAS to Call Center: Making the Big Move." Here she gave specific details to DeHaan's broad vision to migrate the industry to the next level, which she advocates is a call center. Osmon reassures the industry that they don't need to abandon their traditional TAS clients in order to be successful in the call center environment (Osmon, 1997, p. 1).

Although many significant similarities exist between an answering service and a call center (staffing, computers, telephony, etc.) differences exist in the scope of each account, the expectations of the clients, and the marketing and support efforts required (Osmon, 1997, p. 1).

First consider the length of a call. In the TAS business a call is a message and can be counted on to last under 60 seconds. In the call center arena, a call is an order and the length of it increases considerably, starting at about 3 minutes and expanding up to 5 and is in some cases 10 minutes. This necessitates employing entirely different paradigms when projecting traffic needs and the corresponding schedule to meet that projection (Osmon, 1997, p. 1).

The area of customer service is vastly different as well, since call center clients require more interaction, have heightened performance exceptions, and are more quality conscience than the typical TAS client. In fact, Osmon allocates one customer service representative to 1,000 TAS clients but reduces the ratio to 40 when dealing with her "special

31

applications" accounts in her call center. This implies that the call center account needs 25 times the attention of a TAS client (1997, p. 2).

Pricing is another consideration. Osmon bemoans the low prices charged by their TAS competitors and she adamantly warns not to repeat that error when quoting call center prospects. She provides an effective analogy when she asks if one would be more comfortable with a $15 an hour attorney or a $125 an hour alternative. "Enough is enough. We are not a fifty-five dollar a month commodity. That's a cable bill. That's not us. We are people" (1997, p.2).

Her other recommendations include being aware that the TAS industry has a reputation as being the rookies when compared to the direct marketing firms and call centers. Next, secure a contact; do not do any work without a contract or money up front. Informal agreements and a handshake can quickly turn sour on a large, high-volume account should misunderstandings occur. Then, plan for three to six weeks to setup, program, and train on the account. Her final advice is to remain "close to your roots" (Osmon, 1997, p. 5). Realize that the traditional TAS owner/manager makes for an excellent small company entrepreneur; build and capitalize on that reality (pp. 2–5).

TAS According to Michaels

In his article, "How to Start an Answering Service," TAS industry guru, publisher of *Connections Magazine*, and TAS business broker, Steve Michaels (1997c) states that in 1987 there were 4,200 answering services. Together these services billed $900 million a year. This calculates out to an average annual gross revenue of $214,000 per operation. He contrasts these figures to 1995 statistics, when the number of services dropped to 4,100, but total billing increased to $2.4 billion. The average annual gross revenue per answering service figured to be $585,000 in 1995. This is a 173% increase over 1988 levels. It is an increase of 2.6 times in 8 years or an annual growth rate of 15% a year—well ahead of the rate of inflation. Michaels concludes that these statistics (of a decline in the number of services, coupled with a dramatic increase in revenues) are a result of industry consolidations and buyouts (Michaels, 1997, p. 1).

Michaels himself plays a part in both the start of new services and the buyouts of existing ones. [Whether he spotted a trend and pursued it or began the trend to start with is one of conjecture. In actuality, the reality may lie somewhere in between.] He offers advice to those who wish to start a TAS business from scratch and advocates that those in complementary businesses (alarm monitoring and paging) expand into the answering service business. Lastly, he suggests that experienced businesspeople can buy existing services as viable and amply profitable businesses. He points out that it is "always cheaper to buy a service than to start one from scratch" (1997c, p. 1) and further suggests that existing TAS owners buy the accounts of their competitors to increase their operation's scale, efficiency, and profits. The combined impact of Michaels' recommendations is more people entering the industry and many who are already there expanding via acquisition (Michaels, 1997c, pp. 1–11).

Unfortunately, it is generally difficult for an existing answering service to borrow money from a bank to leverage an acquisition. Michaels acknowledges that a TAS is generally "cash heavy, but has little collateral" (1997c, p. 6). He advocates buying services based on a multiple of monthly billing. The multiples range from a low of 3 times (a distressed sale, customer list only) to 15 times (a large service, customers, and equipment). Incidentally, Michaels classifies a large service as one with more than $50,000 in monthly revenues, which is $600,000 annually. Typical payment arrangements are 20 to 30% down with the balance over two to five years, depending on size. An alternative method is to pay a percentage of receivables over a period of time. Occasionally cash sales do occur, but at a lower price. Michaels notes that one should expect a 20% loss of clients during an acquisition (1997c, pp. 6–8; 1997b, p. 3).

In his companion article, "How Not to Sell Your Telephone Answering Service," Michaels (1997b) adds that there currently exists a wide array of telephone answering services. At one end of the spectrum is the lone person working out of their home, under-capitalized and using obsolete equipment. Contrast that with the other extreme of a sophisticated, high-tech endeavor which is computerized, employing paperless messaging (that is, the messages are typed into a computer versus being handwritten) and allowing a multitude of companion and ancillary services to be offered. These supplemental services include voice mail, alpha numeric paging, fax delivery, and email delivery. While modern, up-to-date equipment is essential to meet the expectations of most TAS clients, Michaels points out that equipment is generally not an issue during a sale, as "84% of all existing TAS buyers buy the accounts only" (1997b, p. 1–4).

In a back page "advertorial," which Michaels (1997a) sometimes runs in his Connections Magazine, he proclaims, "It's no secret that there are buyers looking for large profitable bureaus [answering services] to acquire," (outside, back cover). He indicates that he encountered several such individuals at the ATSI trade show in 1997. They are in an aggressive acquisition mode. Michaels was unsure of how long this buy cycle would last and noted that there was a limited number of ideal acquisition candidates and a finite amount of investment capital with which to purchase them. He did not speculate how long to expect their acquisition sprees would last or "when the scarcity of high-paying buyers will dry up" (outside, back cover).

"America is buying and selling businesses at an astounding rate" (Knowledge, p. 6) according to a July 1997 article in Business Opportunity Journal, which was reprinted in Michaels' Connections Magazine. The unidentified author concurs with Michaels that buying an established business is easier and increases the success rate. The author also recommends to, "begin to position the business for sale from the day it is purchased," (Knowledge, p. 7). There is also a final warning for those who are currently in the sell mode, noting that it is typical for an owner's attention to his business to decrease and become diverted once he is in a sell mode. This is a mistake, since not only can the value of the business decline during this time of neglect, but also the deal can fall through, leaving an inattentive owner with a business he is no longer interested in (Knowledge, pp. 6–7).

The aforementioned connection Michaels sees between the paging and answering service industry is echoed by Motorola's Jim Page. In his article, "Paging and the TAS industry: An Opportunity for Synergy," Page (1997) forecasts that paging could be an opportunity for growth within the TAS industry in the nineties. Paging is growing at 20% a year and the fastest growing segment of paging is alphanumeric paging. (Alphanumeric paging allows a text message to be displayed on a pager, as opposed to other types which display a number, receive a short voice message, or merely beep.) The dilemma with alphanumeric paging is the absence of a ubiquitous data input terminal to send the text message. While a voice page can be sent by simply calling the pager number and speaking the message, and a digital page sent by again calling the pager number and entering a callback number on the numeric pad of the telephone, there is no easy way to enter a text message from a telephone; a computer or other device with a keyboard and modem is required. The telephone answering service is perfectly positioned to fill the void. Not only do they have computers to send the message, but they have staff to enter it, telephone lines for the senders to call, and they are available twenty-four hours a day. Page envisions the TAS as a system integrator, combining the pager, paging system, and their telephony infrastructure into a seamless service offering for the paging customer: call a number, leave a message, and the message is displayed on the pager. Future growth in the wireless communications industry combined with the emerging information services will work together to push the concept to the next level (Page, 1997, pp. 1–3).

Paging notwithstanding, Michaels has taken decisive action in regard to the synergy he sees between the alarm industry and the TAS industry. The *Connections Magazine* which he publishes is sent free to qualified individuals in the TAS and related industries. The circulation of 32,000 was recently increased by 7,000, expanding it to 39,000, when a mailing list was obtained of alarm companies with "manned monitoring stations" (Connections, 1997, p. 41). These companies are ideal candidates to expand into the TAS business because they are already staffed twenty-four hours a day—one of the most problematic aspects of the TAS industry (Connections, 1997, p. 41). This strategic move by Michaels increases the potential pool of buyers considering telephone answering services as acquisition or expansion possibilities.

Oliver Shatz, another industry influencer, agrees with Michaels in many areas. His article, "TAS is Back!" documents both areas of agreement and divergence. He concurs with Michaels that the number of telephone answering services has decreased in the last ten years. However, where Michaels' figures calculate the actual decrease at about 5%, Shatz uses the subjective adjective "dramatic" to suggest a much greater degree of shrinkage (1996, p. 12). He indicates that the size of the market has decreased as a result of "mergers and entrepreneurial fatigue" (p. 12). This is a normal fluctuation that all industries go through, which Michaels also acknowledges (Michaels, 1997a, outside back cover). Shatz believes that the TAS market is now on the upswing, with "the actual number of answering services on the rise" (p. 12). [This is a claim Michaels is yet to make]. Shatz's reasons for this growth are numerous. One such explanation is a regenerated demand for live services as a result of backlash against voice mail and more specifically, automated attendant systems. A second reason is greatly increased competition in the order-taking business, which he states was held in virtual monopoly by "13 non-TAS companies" as little as "five years ago" (p. 12). Another reason is that answering services are capturing the attention of savvy entrepreneurs, who are attracted to the cash flow potential, "small space requirements," insignificant perishables, low utility costs, and inexpensive insurance (p. 12). Lastly, renewed interest in the American dream of owning a business, by a disillusioned and downsized corporate America, is enticing and fascinating a new set of entrepreneurs and business managers. Shatz concludes by admitting that, "there may never be the same amount of telephone answering services that there were in the mid-eighties, but they are making a comeback" (pp. 12–14).

Shatz's comments appeared in the winter 1996 issue of *The Communicator*, a short-lived publication geared toward the TAS industry. In the same issue of *The Communicator*, a companion article appeared by an unidentified author [likely the editorial staff] confirming many of Shatz's statements. Entitled, "Don't Sell Yourself Short," the article addressed issues of interest to those who might be in the market to sell their telephone answering service. It began by acknowledging that the sale price of answering services has dropped 40% in recent years. This is attributed to lowered expectations by buyers, and hence their ensuing offers, as to an actual change in the value of these services. Buyers who pay a percentage of actual future collections were chastised as the culprits of these lowered valuations and selling prices. It was pointed out that in these "percent of collections" scenarios, the seller assumes all risk whereas the buyer assumes virtually no risk (Don't, 1996, p. 5). The perception that a seller needed to sell within the industry was also debunked as mythology, stating that many of those looking to go into business see real advantages of owning a telephone answering service as opposed to, say a restaurant or dry cleaner. The conclusion was clear, "Remember that answering services are making a comeback and there is more value in your business than you may think" (Don't, 1996, p. 7).

The Association of California Enhanced Telemessaging Services (ACETS) concurs with Shatz's aforementioned take on the backlash against voice mail. According to ACETS (1997), the introduction of voice mail services in the nineteen-eighties caused great alarm and concern in the industry. Those who owned operator-based answering services felt that the low-cost, automated voice mail version of "answering service" would siphon off clients in vast numbers. They feared that the industry would be decimated and possibly eventually wiped out (ACETS, p. 2).

An often-criticized form of voice mail service is called automated attendant. Automated attendant systems prompt the caller to press specific buttons on their telephone to route their call to the appropriate person or department. In many cases this caused a certain level of frustration among callers. "This," according to ACETS, "led to a swing in the pendulum, back to Operator services" [sic] (ACETS, 1997, p. 2).

ACETS concludes decisively by saying, "The element of human-touch, and compassion cannot be duplicated electronically. This is the key to the survival of our industry" (ACETS, 1997, p. 2). Quite simply, the staff of a telephone answering service is the industry's competitive edge. Additionally, the live service can also be combined successfully with small portions of automated voice mail service to provide a humanly acceptable level of service for a more cost-effective price (ACETS, 1997, p. 2).

BCSI and OPXPO

In 1996 a new trade association was formed. They call themselves BCSI, which stands for Business Communications Services International. BCSI self-proclaims themselves as a "trade association for the Communications Services bureau and reseller" (BCSI, 1997, p. 1). They define the direction of their organization "as the association for anyone and any business that sells communications services, principally to the business market" (p.1) Their target membership list largely backs this all-inclusive ambition and is a widely divergent group of communications related industries. It is comprised of "telephone answering services," "independent voice mail companies," "paging and cellular resellers," "video teleconferencing services companies," "independent representatives for communications services," "long distance services," "call centers, executive suites, and anyone providing technology, services, or products to the industry" (p. 1).

Reviewing the services offered by the board of directors' own companies reveals a somewhat less divergent membership (assuming that the board reflects a cross section of the membership.) Of the eleven-member board, all eleven indicate they are in the "voice processing [that is, voice mail] business." Eight are also in the telephone answering business and five of those are also call centers. No one indicated they were a call center and not a telephone answering service. Other services offered by board members include paging, internet, and cellular. None of the board was in the executive suite, long distance, or video teleconferencing business (BCSI, 1997, p. 5–6). As such it appears that the board is heavily represented by members of the TAS industry. Still, despite this obvious imbalance, BCSI is more divergent than and encompasses a greater demographic than the traditional TAS industry associations (ATSI, industry user groups, and the state and regional associations). As such it is expected that BCSI will collectively have differing perspectives and a broader view than those advocated within the industry (p. 5–6).

BCSI members enjoy several benefits of membership. These include a "monthly marketing program offering," a member newsletter called TeleTips, the availability of low-cost errors and omissions insurance, a resource letter called Communications trends, and an annual convention; it is called OPXPO (BCSI, 1997, 2–4).

At the 1996 OPXPO convention a panel discussion was held entitled, "Designing the Telecommunications Center of the Future." The panel discussion was made into a pair of articles and published in *Connections Magazine* in 1997. The four panelists were Frank D'Ascenzo of Axon Communications, Barb Willis of Converse/Startel, Jack Baldwin of Cad Com, and Donna West of Focus Communications (Michaels C., 1997a, p. 1 & 1997b, p. 1). The first three are TAS industry vendors and the latter a successful answering service owner.

The springboard question for the panel was, "How can a telephone answering service position itself so that it can move into the future and take advantage of the opportunities available?" The secondary questions were, "How do we position our business to take advantage of this?" and "Where is the road going to lead us and how are we going to get there from here?" (Michaels C., 1997a, p. 1 & 1997b, p. 1).

Barb Willis of Comverse recommended that one should first look at the history of one's business. What are the business's assets and liabilities? Then, once that has been determined, look for ways to build upon and increase the assets and simultaneously seek to minimize the liabilities

(Michaels, C. 1997a, p. 1).

According to Willis, one weakness (liability) of the industry is ineffective sales and marketing. Historically, an answering service would merely place a display ad or even line listing in the local yellow pages and wait for the phone to ring. Virtually all sales efforts were reactive in nature. Conversely, Willis states that the industry's key asset is and has been its telephone service representatives. She then cautions that any given service is only as good as its worst employee. "It all comes back to operator services. The answering service industry is not going away. The business is changing, and each business must prepare for the upcoming changes and needs to take advantage of the presented opportunities" (Michaels, C. 1997a, p. 2). Her conclusion is that it is, therefore, imperative to carefully examine how services are marketed and the need for a direct proactive sales staff (Michaels, C. 1997a, 1–2 & 1997b, p. 46).

Willis went on to give some concrete ideas of service possibilities. The first was offering first level help desks to local corporations. By using software available today, answers to common questions or problems can be programmed for easy and effective access by TSRs (Telephone Service Representatives). This would be a great offering to market to service companies. Next, she suggested handling messaging for corporate sales departments. Take their messages and send them anywhere in the world: fax, email, alphanumeric pager, etc. (Michaels, C., 1997b, p. 46).

"Probably one of the biggest words today in large corporations is outsourcing," Willis continued. "Corporations realize that they can't do all things and be successful; they realize the value of a message" (p.

46). When corporations outsource, they seek consistency and quality. One type of basic outsourcing is called "remote receptionists." Fortune 500 companies are willing to pay thousands of dollars a month to have their calls answered and transferred or a message taken. They will outsource this if it can save them money and still provide the quality of service that they need (Michaels, C., 1997b, p. 46).

Frank D'Ascenzo of Axon Communications was next to give his comments. D'Ascenzo says that the types of services that can be offered in the future will be a function of the technology which has been selected and implemented. The basic TAS system will serve as the basis for this technology, therefore it is important to select this equipment with great care and thought. A significant advance in technology in recent years has been open architecture systems. This becomes even more important when one considers the increased prevalence of local area networks, wide area networks, and the network of networks—the internet. These developments call for a new technology paradigm away from single vendor solutions of proprietary systems towards open systems running on commercially available computers and telephony switches. With such a paradigm it makes sense to work with a systems integrator as opposed to a single vendor. This allows for a wider, less restrictive choice of vendors, systems, software, and solutions. D'Ascenzo went on to state how his company was following this new technology paradigm (Michaels, C. 1997a, p. 2–5).

The next panel member to address the attendees was another equipment vendor, Jack Baldwin, President and owner of Cad Com. Baldwin also approached the future of the industry from a technical perspective. He concurred with D'Ascenzo on the need to have open architecture systems. Baldwin's comments were as much visionary as they were pragmatic. He first stated that he foresaw close interaction in the future between the telephone and television industries. This convergence, as others have called it, is readily evidenced by the telephone companies getting involved in, merging with, or acquiring cable businesses. A key reason is that cable television is migrating from coaxial to fiber optics. "What we are looking at," Baldwin stated, "is an integration of video, phones and television, all in the sale fiber optic cabling." He predicted that the next generation of phones would have video as well as audio. Correspondingly, clients will be able to see TSRs as well as talk to them (Michaels, C., 1997b, p. 12).

Baldwin also addressed email as a future opportunity for the TAS industry. He envisions accessing a client's email and converting it to a page, a fax, or a text message to relay to the client. He then went on to predict a wireless phone system, such as is currently available in Europe, to make mobile two-way communication available and affordable. In conclusion, Baldwin saw that, "today's answering service will evolve over the next couple of years into a communications center." They must specialize and find a market niche. Once the niche has been found, they must provide service better than anyone else in order to keep that niche as a competitive advantage (Michaels, C., 1997b, p. 12).

The final panelist to talk was Donna West. West, duly noted that all the other panelists advocated the "need to spend some serious money." Since most in the audience were not likely ready for that, West instructed them to go home and raise their rates. She suggested giving some of that increased revenue to their TSR staff in the form of greater compensation. Because of all the increased future opportunities, more will be demanded of the staff. By paying them more, she implied, more capable staff could be attracted to meet the servicing requirements of the future. She concluded, "Stop undervaluing what we do ... we have operator services that will never go away" (Michaels, C., 1997b, p. 12).

The executive director of BCSI is Roy Emmet. Emmet is also President of Vital Communications, Inc. which offers consulting for voice/fax processing service bureaus (Emmet, 1997b, p. 5). Emmet wrote an article in the aforementioned *Connections Magazine*. His article title asked the question, "What Will the New Communications Service Bureau of the Late 90's Be Like?" Emmet begins by stating the obvious, that the business world is changing. He adds that a big part of that change is communications related (Emmet, 1997b, p. 1 & 5).

By applying logic and experience, Emmet says one can determine that prospects for communication services are simply in search of help. They want to streamline their business, reduce overhead, keep up with how others are communicating, run their business better, and gain new customers. Traditional solutions do not meet the need they are looking to fill; they want modern, future-focused solutions, but not so visionary as to be impractical or unusable (Emmet, 1997b, p. 1).

Who can meet this need and rise to the challenge? Emmet points out that the only candidates with any sort of long-term track record are those whose roots are in the telephone answering service industry. He sees a niche which will evolve into being a "professional communications consultant." Those who embark on such a course will find that it "bare[s] little resemblance to the answering service of today" (1997b, p. 2). Unlike other advocates in the TAS industry, however, Emmet does not view the twenty-four hours a day, seven days a week (24 by 7), live operator as a cornerstone for his future vision, but rather that the key component is a "feature rich, commercial grade voice and fax processing system" (1997b, p. 2). Pressures of cost, efficiency, and automation are forces which will make this paradigm shift a reality (1997b, pp. 1–2).

Rather, he sees "specially trained operators [as] an additional engine for this hybrid service bureau" (Emmet, 1997b, p. 2) and admits that some bureaus will not even have service staff (that is, operators). Such an equipped business will be able to offer a full range of communications services from twenty-four-hour messaging, information services by fax, audio, internet, and soon video. Other options would include automated order-taking, literature request lines, and automated sales presentations. By partnering with other businesses, paging, cellular, long distance, and 800 numbers can also be offered to produce one-stop shopping for virtually all communication needs. Their target market will be home-based businesses, the virtual corporation, and advertising and marketing companies. "Service bureaus that redirect their efforts this way," Emmet concludes, "can expect to be leaders in a volatile new dimension on the world of communication" (1997b, p. 2–4).

The vision Emmet advocates corresponds to the consulting services that he offers. A more moderate, but similarly slanted article, by Emmet, later appeared in *Connections Magazine*. Under the heading of "Future Trends," Emmet's (1997) subtitle proclaims, "We Have Special Business Solutions Unavailable from Any Other Communications Companies." Emmet again refers to the significant changes which have occurred in the communications industry in the past ten years. "It is impossible," he states, "for businesses to grasp what all is in front of them." This presents a significant opportunity for the telephone answering service industry. Namely, to present one's business "as true, personalized resources to provide special communications applications that are not available from other sources." Emmet can think of no businesses, other than telephone answering services, which do this on a local level (p. 16).

Emmet sees the telephone answering service industry as having two prime assets which properly position it for this opportunity. The first is the telephone service representative staff and the second is automated services capability. "Nobody has this one-two punch but you who are in the business" (p. 16). The problem he asserts is that answering centers and call centers are planning on growing by geographic expansion and will continue to offer traditional answering service or order-taking service as a primary service. Instead, their attention should be "spent in [their] own local markets to seek out more in-depth clients with specialized, full-service solutions" (p. 22). The obvious start is to sell additional services to one's existing client base. Look for niches which are already being served and expand them. The next step is to seek referrals from existing clients. He also encourages brainstorming and looking for services which are not offered by other companies (Emmet, 1997a, pp. 16, 22, 41).

Views From the Call Center/Telemarketing Industry

By expanding the scope of the search to another level, the call center and inbound telemarketing industries can be explored for relevant information and alternative perspectives.

An article which originally appeared in *Telecommunications Magazine* in June 1997 was obtained at their internet web site. The article, written by Bob St. Ledger addresses issues which face call centers today and gives insight to telephone answering services which wish to migrate in that direction. St. Ledger begins by stating that, "The power of call centers to improve business processes is expanding" (p. 1). At one time a screen pop (that is instantaneously displaying information about a call when it is answered) was all the technology needed to meet the needs of clients and their callers. Today call centers must deal with higher expectations from their callers, which means that they need to anticipate the potential for higher customer dissatisfaction. To address this, they should look at activities which proceed and follow the actual phone call itself. The goal should be to streamline and more fully integrate all these tasks into the call center's functions (p. 1).

Skills-based routing is a significant development which can improve customer satisfaction. Skills-based routing allows the call to be directed to the most available person who is knowledgeable and trained to handle the needs of the caller. The methodologies used to determine how the call will be routed includes database searches, DNIS, ANI, and DTMF notification (from an automated attendant). Situations when skills-based routing can be used are to select agents to match the language of the caller, their geographic region, or the type of product they are calling about. Skills-based routing, coupled with a single toll-free number allows callers to have the perception of one-stop shopping. This greatly increases customer satisfaction and decreases frustration of needing to call different numbers based on a particular need. At times when the telephone service representative who answers the phone cannot meet the need of the callers, the goal should be to transfer the call only once, to the appropriate person, and to send with the call the account information and the data already obtained from the caller. This requires a computer network which is integrated into the phone system (St. Ledger, 1997, pp. 1–2).

For more complex issues, case-based routing must be used. Case-based routing is an expert systems technology which prompts the TSR to ask certain predefined questions, the answer to each question branches in a different direction to quickly and effectively handle the caller's needs. The benefits of case-based routing are shorter call times and the requirement for less training. These benefits provide better service to callers and reduce the expenses of the call center (St. Ledger, 1997, p. 3).

Another method of reducing call center calls and increasing customer satisfaction is to make call center information and solutions available on the World Wide Web. St. Ledger also includes monitoring software as a tool to increase customer satisfaction. Typically monitoring techniques included listening to TSRs and gathering statistics about their performance. This needs to be replaced by software that allows TSRs to not only track their own performance, but to also compare it with their counterparts. By properly using monitoring in a constructive fashion, not only can quality be improved, but turnover can be reduced. Again, these benefits positively impact both the caller and the call center (St. Ledger, 1997, pp. 3–4).

The eighty-year-old Direct Marketing Association (DMA) has a long history of helping, first those in direct mail, and later all those involved in all forms of marketing. An increasingly growing aspect of marketing is the role played by the telephone in moving the marketing process forward or making the sale. The DMA's Web site offers useful information in this regard. Their article, "Making the Most of an Effective Medium: DMA's Guidelines for Marketing by Telephone" provides a wealth of general information that would be of interest to many telephone answering services. First the DMA defines telemarketing. Telemarketing is "the structured use of the telephone to purchase or sell products or services, to obtain or give information to businesses and residences, or to solicit funds or support for charities" (Making, 1997, p. 1). This is a wide, far-reaching viewpoint which by definition encompasses all telephone answering services and virtually all the services they offer.

To further clarify the issue, the DMA divides telemarketing into inbound and outbound. Inbound telemarketing includes, "programs [which] enable consumers to call companies to place orders or receive products, services, or charitable information" (Making, 1997, p. 1). The key point here is that it is the consumer who initiates contact and the call center who reacts. Conversely, outbound telemarketing is where "companies call customers and potential customers to inform them of offers that may be of interest, to provide service information, or to raise funds" (p. 1). Here the opposite is true, where the call center is proactive, and the customer or prospect is reactive. It is outbound telemarketing which has stirred the ire of the public and received the bad press. Whereas inbound telemarketing is a huge benefit to consumers, allowing them to be in control when they choose to shop by telephone and obtain product information. Inbound telemarketing by definition is what telephone answering services do; outbound telemarketing is a different alternative which could be considered as another service offering or as a totally new direction.

The DMA offers guidelines for marketing by telephone. These are a group of standards which the DMA advocates for their members and the industry as a whole. Most of the guideline's thirteen articles specifically relate to those doing outbound telemarketing, however, some also apply to inbound telemarketing as well. The DMA Web site also recommends other sources of information which provide similar information (Making, 1997, 1–6).

Another source of information is *Service Level Newsletter*. This newsletter, and the organization behind it, focuses completely on the inbound side of telemarketing and as such is another excellent resource for the telephone answering service. Their May 1995 article, "Call Center Consolidations: Questions to Ask, Pitfalls to Avoid" is especially relevant given the recent wave of consolidations and acquisitions within the telephone answering service industry. The article's author, Bill Church is CEO of Call Center Enterprises, which helps large companies develop huge call centers. Church states that "improved technology and corporate reengineering have accelerated a trend toward consolidating call centers," but he warns, "consolidation isn't right for every organization" (p. 8). In fact, less than fifty percent of all call center consolidations are ever successful at reaching the goals they had originally established (p. 8).

Traditional wisdom and queue theory (as in, "all other representatives are busy assisting other callers, please stay on the line") is that the largest possible group of agents, handling the largest queue of calls is the most efficient. Church confirms the truth in that but cautions that mere efficiency alone may not be the right answer in all situations. There are three key questions to be considered before jumping headlong into a consolidation effort. First, have practices and procedures been standardized in the centers to be consolidated? If the different centers do the same task, but in different ways, conflict and problems are bound to result. Next, do those involved in making the decision comprehend the initial human impact on the employees? Many employees would need to be laid off; those keeping their jobs would need to be relocated and reassigned, possibly needing to learn new skills or assume new positions. Lastly, has the cost of the integration been carefully considered. While it is true that long-term savings will occur, there still will be an initial increase in costs to make the consolidation happen. These costs include not only capital expenses facilities and equipment, but also include training, consulting, and increased management requirements (Church, 1997, pp. 8–9).

Once a decision has been made to proceed with a call center integration, Church advocates careful planning as a key to a successful consolidation. "It requires you to rethink your business (1997, p. 9). Next, make sure that generic systems are in place to replace the familiar and likely undocumented information that resides in the TSRs heads. In the same vein, most organizations have an informal "sneaker-net" that is used to find information and get things done. For example, if there is a question to ask someone, simply walk over to them and ask. But what if, because of the consolidation, suddenly that person is in another location hundreds of miles away, how will the question be communicated? How long will it take to get a response? This issue directly impacts responsiveness to the callers and overall call center efficiency. Next it is time to re-educate the TSRs. The goal should be to make the entire staff work and think as one. Take what is good and works from each call center; do not assume that one does everything right and has a corner on success. Failure to do so can result in "us versus them" mentalities and cause internal infighting and confrontations. Church concludes his advice, saying that, "While consolidating call centers can be painful and time-consuming, the rewards can be great in the right situation. Careful planning and up-front work contribute greatly to the likelihood of success" (Church, 1997, p. 8–9).

Jim Nash (1997), in writing for *CIO* magazine, also recognizes the growing importance of call centers. In his October first article, "Fast Fone Farms, Fat Profits," he states, "The once humble call center is taking on strategic importance with the convergence of helpdesk, telesales and customer service operations" (p. 40). First, Nash defines a phone farm as "a reference to the dense concentration of employee cubicles in large call centers" (p. 40). He adds, that call centers have "become a nexus of sophisticated new information systems" (p. 40). Nash provides case studies of three companies who realized the importance of call centers to their operations, and he shares some of their thoughts, ideas, and paradigms. The companies profiled were HFS Inc. (Ramada Inn, Howard Johnson, etc.), Metropolitan Life Insurance Company, and Apple Computer (p. 40).

According to Nash, HFS officials stated that call centers were one of the methods they successfully used to build their company and help it grow. Realizing the importance of the call center to the company's growth and success, and the fact that their call center needs were increasing faster than they could react, they chose early on to plan proactively for the future. They selected a middle ground in the debate about outsourcing, taking a compromise approach, deciding to partner with another company whose annual business cycle complemented theirs, allowing for overflow calls of one company to be outsourced to the other company who was at their seasonal low. Six months later the cycles would reverse, allowing calls to overflow in the other direction. At the time of his article Nash did not know how this arrangement worked out, but it is an example of creative solutions to dealing with seasonal fluctuations in call center traffic (Nash, 1997, pp. 40, 42, 46, 50).

At Metropolitan Life, CIO Jim Logan embarked on a "campaign called Once and Done" (Nash, 1997, p. 42). It signals the company's goal of handling a call one time, not needing to call back, processing it correctly, and doing so without the need to transfer it. Logan indicates that this campaign will enhance the company's image with its customers and that doing so was important since the call centers were increasingly becoming a primary point of contact with clients. MetLife's V.P. of call center operations adds, "To a large extent, in any business, product price and quality can be readily duplicated. Therefore, customer service will increasingly differentiate competitors" (Nash, 1997, p. 46). Along these lines, MetLife's goal is for their call center staff to handle ninety percent of all calls without transferring them (Nash, 1997, pp. 42, 46, 48).

Unlike Nash's first two examples, Apple Computer's call centers were having a customer satisfaction problem which was in need of drastic resolution. The short version of their solution was that they turned to their Information Systems department for assistance to integrate and implement new technology. This solution was consistent with the paradigms of the corporate office at Apple who "feel its call center information systems are a strategic strength, not the operators themselves" (Nash, 1997, p. 52). This is exactly the opposite of the feeling at MetLife, who believe they must maintain total control of what is being said by their call center representatives to their customers. As such, it is not unexpected that MetLife does not see call center outsourcing as appropriate for customer service issues. Again, Apple takes the opposite view, concluding that it is less costly to outsource the call center (Nash, 1997, p. 50, 52).

David Cooperstein, an analyst with Forrester Research Inc.'s Telecom Strategies, writes in *CIO* magazine that call center managers need to not overlook the importance of the internet in their operations. In his article, "Click Here for an Agent" Cooperstein quotes Forrester's estimates that in 1997 call centers handle ninety-five percent of the billions of customer interactions that take place. The remaining five percent are handled by email and letters. Today's penetration of email is at fifteen percent; in just four years it is predicted to reach fifty percent; it is reasonable to expect that customer interactions will increase proportionally. Couple this trend with the reality that customers are becoming increasingly frustrated with IVR (Interactive Voice Response) and voice mail. Still these technologies are continuing to be implemented, so it is expected that as customers look for acceptable alternatives, they will turn to email. Unfortunately, laments Cooperstein, "call center managers are virtually ignoring the internet" (1997, p. 36). Companies with Web sites are not effectively linking them to their call centers. Additionally, call center interactions with customers via email lack a standard procedure. With a low volume of email this is not a critical issue, but as email usage increases, this lack of process becomes problematic (1997, p. 36).

"Forrester expects the role of call centers will change from large-scale telephony exchanges to customer interaction centers" (Cooperstein, 1997, p. 37). They define customer interaction centers as "the people and technology that will handle remote customer communications, using telephony, the internet, and other media" (Cooperstein, 1997, p. 37). Toward that end, Cooperstein defines a new term, "teleweb," which is "the interaction of Web sites with the call center at the click of a mouse button" (1997, p. 37). To deal with these rapidly developing trends, call center managers must begin planning for them now. This will include technology to manage the flow of email, systems to handle the connection of "call me back" buttons on web sites, as well as allowing agent and customer to interact simultaneously on the same Web page (Cooperstein, 1997, pp. 37–38).

Cooperstein makes three recommendations for call centers to prepare for these internet eventualities. First, run a trial teleweb for direct sales. Next, increase the standards when hiring call center employees. Lastly, establish an email center (which will be to email like a call center is to the telephone). Those leading the pack, concludes Cooperstein, "will embrace the call center as the epitome of their 'technology meets the consumer' customer-focused organization" (Cooperstein, 1997, pp. 37–38).

Relevant General Business Literature

There is a vast array of general business literature that is applicable to and builds upon the thoughts and ideas already expounded. To cover all such works would be an insurmountable task and take inexhaustible effort. Therefore, only selected works will be covered, which are deemed to be more relevant than others.

Ian Morrison's book, *The Second Curve: Managing the Velocity of Change* was briefly summarized in *Inc.* magazine (1996). "Morrison writes that businesses must change from traditional operating models to forms that deal with new technologies, new customers, and new markets" (p. 18). This certainly implies agreement with Cooperstein's previous comments on proactively embracing the internet.

Morrison's directive is to stop selling solutions and to start finding answers with customers. As an example, consider how many temporary help firms have co-located offices with their larger customers, literally setting up shop inside their customer's facility. The recommendation on how small companies should think is to focus on the irrational and inefficient aspects found in almost every business and look for ways to exploit them. By following the process from start to finish (from origin to the customer) look for ways where technology can change or enhance the process and cause a strategic advantage. The technologies to consider? A PC and the internet (Morrison, 1996, p. 18).

In another *Inc.* magazine contribution, Jim Collins, co-author of the book, "Built to Last," discussed the three characteristics that enduring companies should possess. The first is "It's not what you make, it's what you stand for" (Collins, 1997, p. 42). Compare Zenith and

Motorola. Both made televisions. Zenith continued to focus on what they made (televisions), whereas Motorola focused on what they stood for ("applying technology to benefit the public"). The second quality is "forget strategy, build mechanisms instead" (p. 45). Mechanisms allow one to promote purpose and stay focused. Consider one of 3M's famous mechanisms to nurture innovation, which simply directs employees to spend fifteen percent of their time working on whatever they want to. Lastly is "the death of the charismatic leader and the birth of an architect" (p. 48). Any company that is to last cannot depend on a single inspiring person to lead and guide it. Rather, the smart leader will build mechanisms which will promote core values (pp. 41–50).

Business Expansion

Expanding via acquisition has already been discussed. This, however, is but one method of business growth. Philip Orsino's book *Successful Business Expansion* (1994) lists several other types of expansion options. In addition to growth through acquisition, there is also growth through merger, start-up, internal growth, vertical integration, and horizontal expansion (p. 17).

Of all the expansion options listed, expanding internally is the easiest to pursue. Basically, this involves creating or adding value for existing clients, improving marketing efforts, and extending product lines. Adding value can be done by using technology to increase quality. "Computer technology and electronics are helping to create better quality products [services], and the goal of business is to have the most efficient operations possible" (p. 64). Add to this, being a low-cost producer and the result is a strong defensive position against competitive pressures. Being a low-cost provider is not only getting materials (that is, equipment and telephony services) at a low cost, but "also means obtaining labor at the best price" (p.65). Another point is to create value through innovation. In the area of marketing, Orsino states the insightfully obvious, "Anyone who sells anything can sell more through improved marketing" (p. 66). To do this, first, stay close to clients and demonstrate that proximity is a benefit resulting in better service. Then gather information about competitors, amass knowledge about the industry, and think in terms of the needs of the clients. These directives will point the way toward improved marketing (pp. 63–77).

Growing internally is a defensive strategy for growth, a more offensive approach to growth is to enter new markets, franchise, or form

strategic alliances. Of these, entering new markets is the most germane
to telephone answering services. In considering expanding into new
markets, Orsino advises to, "think nationally, act regionally" (p. 81).
Realize that even within the United States cultural differences exist
from region to region which need to be considered and accommodated.
Also, first target those markets which are geographically close
by. This allows for regional strength to be developed without
the danger of spreading the business too thinly over a dispersed
geographic area. Once the right new market has been identified,
careful market analysis and research is required before rash expansion
begins. Learn about the competition, the commercial base, demand,
existing infrastructures [telephony infrastructure], labor issues, and
tax issues. A less costly method of geographic expansion is franchising.
"Franchising is essentially a way to expand by using other people's
money," and "there is very little that can't be franchised" (p. 86).
The advantages of franchising are rapid expansion at low cost with
reduced managerial demands when compared to company owned
expansion. The downside of franchising is a loss of control over quality
and dealing with unsuccessful franchisees. Expanding via strategic
alliances is a middle ground between self-growth and franchising.
Successful alliances require a change in attitude which is often the
biggest roadblock to implementation and success (Orsino, 1994, pp.
79–100).

The last main category is expansion using acquisition or merger. Why
consider this option? Because claims Orsino, "your future may depend
on it" (p. 103). The benefits of such action are increased efficiency,
savings, and profitability, long-term viability, and greater strength and
vitality. However, be aware that, "Acquisitions and mergers are often

pursued because at least one of the partners forecasts that it won't do as well in the future as it did in the past" (p. 103). Before taking this step, realize that it is much like a marriage, and can suffer from the same maladies, such as a short courtship, poor planning or communications, and a culture clash. Continuing with the marriage analogy, Orsino talks about the courtship phase (a cursory review), the engagement (letter of intent, valuing the company, and due diligence), the ceremony (saying 'I do'), and making the marriage last (communication, planning, and implementation) (Orsino, 1994, pp. 101–127).

"Expanding puts your company at risk," maintains Orsino. "Doing nothing also puts your company at risk, probably greater risk" (p. 204). To manage that risk, carefully evaluate the company's management team and structure; make sure that employees buy into and accept the expansion plan. It is also recommended to upgrade accounting systems and make sure that the needed financial platform is in place prior to embarking on any type of business expansion (Orsino, 1994, pp. 198–205).

Orsino lists nine possible benefits of expansion, which are that it: (1) boosts profitability, (2) helps reduce risk, (3) increases understanding of the industry, (4) increases leverage in distribution channels, (5) helps ensure business survival, (6) makes a company better, (7) helps cut costs, (8) improves efficiency, and (9) keeps companies from being left behind (Orsino, 1994, pp. 2–3).

Before pursuing business expansion, however, consider the costs. "If you are contemplating growth as a way to solve problems," warns Orsino, "don't, because it won't" (p. 14). In fact, plan on growth causing many problems and realize that the bottom line may not be immediately positively impacted. Conversely, not to dissuade growth, Orsino states, "Companies don't fail because they grow. They fail because they don't plan their growth. In fact, it is more likely that a North American company will fail because it doesn't grow than because it does grow" (p. 2). It boils down to growing at a controlled rate, not flat-out expansion just for the sake of growth. "If successful growth depends on planning, successful planning depends on careful self-assessment, (p. 4). "Make no mistake about it," Orsino warns, "expansion changes your company" (p. 4). It requires time, money, and effort; the demands of which are felt by the whole company (pp. 3–9).

To accurately assess the feasibility of business expansion, Orsino outlines ten characteristics of a company that would likely be successful in expansion. It: (1) thinks like a bigger company, (2) sees adjoining markets as potential markets, (3) has a proven ability in strategic planning, (4) prepares and follows written business plans, (5) knows its strengths and weaknesses, (6) is meeting current demand for its products and services, (7) has sound system, financial, and human resources, (8) sees changes as a challenge, (9) looks at growth as a way to strengthen the business, not solve problems, and (10) has analyzed how the expansion will impact the current operation (p. 17).

Orsino states that eight essential ingredients are required of a company for successful expansion:

1. There is a commitment to growing; it cannot happen accidentally.

2. It has knowledge of the industry and economy, for knowledge is power.

3. It is adaptable with plans and procedures.

4. The company has financing, which Orsino calls a resource. "If it's scarce, it's like running out of inventory" (p. 22).

5. It can successfully communicate reassurance to all those impacted by the change.

6. It has the right people and management team in place.

7. It has capacity. Sometimes increases in scale do not translate to increased efficiency, at worst it actually decreases efficiency.

8. It has time and patience; "all growth requires the resources of time and patience" (p. 29) (Orsino, 1994, pp. 17–30).

Of these, financing (as previously mentioned) is more troublesome for answering services (Michaels, 1997c, p. 6) than many of the other items on the list. Orsino, covers several options for funding. These are private equity financing (venture capitalists, angel investors, etc.), mergers (which typically are stock deals), franchising (which allows for expansion using other people's money), debt financing (which Orsino says is risky), and going public. "Public companies have opportunities in equity markets that just don't exist for private companies" (p. 52). These include better access to capital markets, the liquidity of stock (to use stock like money), increased credibility, and a better chance to attract, keep, and motivate employees. However, "taking a company public can be arduous," he warns. "There are many regulatory hoops through which you, your directors, your senior management, and the company will have to jump" (p. 53). "Running a public company," he concludes, "is not for everyone, (p. 55) (Orsino, 1994, 35–59).

Going Public

In preceding sections there was repeated discussion on and references to the topic of buying and selling answering services. These views were all from the perspective of those within or close to the industry, with much of it from Steve Michaels, who among other things, is in the business of being an answering service broker. In a conversation with Michaels, he indicated placing ads in the New York Times to attract interest from the business community to invest in the telephone answering service industry. Some who have seen those ads have acted seriously to adopt Michaels' advice. Informal discussions with some of those individuals, and others who have espoused similar acquisition strategies, have yielded one common thread. That is, regardless of how they selected their acquisitions, how the purchase was structured, what the deal was worth, or the synergistic strategy they pursued, the one area of agreement was to amass a significant portfolio and go public. Although the gross revenue targets varied, the consistent goal was to go public and get rich.

As long as financial markets remain strong and capitalization continues to be in high multiples of gross revenues, going public is a strategy that can be gainfully considered by others as well. In the *Ernst & Young Guide to Taking Your Company Public*, authors Blowers, Erickson, and Milan (1995) detail the pros and cons, ups and downs, and rewards and challenges of taking a business public.

They state that the benefits of being a public company are numerous. The first and most obvious benefit is that selling stock improves the business's financial condition, bringing in money, which does not need to be paid back, and which can be used to retire debt, finance expansion, or fund acquisitions. Going public generally improves the value of the company since the shares are more marketable. A public company projects the perception of maturity and sophistication. Also, more detailed and accurate information is readily available to the investing public. Going public also allows for diversification of personal portfolios and easier estate planning (Blowers et al., 1995, pp. 1–5).

The list of drawbacks is equally significant. First, when going public, there is a risk of losing control if the original owners must sell more than fifty percent of the stock. Correspondingly, the success of the business, which is the profits, must be shared among all shareholders. There is also a loss of privacy as a result of complying with the Securities and Exchange Commission's (SEC) requirements to disclose information about the company, including sales, profit margins, and competitive information. Sensitive information, such as compensation to key employees and benefits and bonus plans are also made public knowledge. This information must be reported on a periodic basis. The time and cost to do so, as well as complying with other SEC requirements, can be significant. In going public management acquires a fiduciary responsibility to shareholders to act in their best interest, of which the prime concern is to provide growth and/or income for the shareholders. It should be noted that there is an increasing willingness on the part of stockholders to take legal action against management when it is deemed that this responsibility has been ignored. Management is also accountable to a board of directors who has authority over many consequential decisions (Blowers et al., 1995, pp. 6–10).

In their book, Blowers et al., guides interested parties through the process of going public, including the preparation, underwriting, registration, offering, and what happens after the offering (1995, pp. 11–110). All these are beyond the immediate concern of this investigation. However, of relevance are considerations in the decision rather to go public. First is timing. Timing the public offering is crucial to success; bad timing will result in an undersubscribed offering, a lower market capitalization (resulting in greater dilution to current owners), or an aborted offering (which still incurs most of the costs). Also, to be contemplated is questioning if a company is ready. Is the company right the size? Investors are generally looking for companies with at least $20 million in revenue and $1 million in net earnings. Next, consider if management is ready. "Can it comfortably adjust to the loss of the relative freedom to act as it sees fit and to the loss of privacy?" (p.13). Can the management team readily adjust to outsiders being involved in making decisions and can management grow as the company grows? A strong management team is a prime consideration for underwriters and investors. Next, investors will look for a track record of consistently high growth and a potential for continued growth in the future. Also, are the company's management and information systems up to the task of timely and accurately making required periodic reports to investors and the SEC? Lastly, investors will also want to know how the proceeds will be used. All these items will be considered as investors and underwriters evaluate a company, which ultimately determines how successful a public offering will be and how much market capitalization is realized (Blowers et al., 1995, pp. 11–16).

If one determines that going public is indeed the path to choose, Blowers et al. warns that preparation should begin at least a year in advance, the company's house should be in order, and to expect a major amount of time and money to be imparted in the process of preparing to go public (1995, pp. 16–19). While the rewards are great, this is not a journey for the uncommitted or faint-hearted (1995, p. 1).

Future Business Predictions and Trends

In a sequel to the highly successful book, *Megatrends*, Naisbitt and Aburdene wrote a follow-up entitled *Megatrends 2000: Ten New Directions for the 1990's*. They write, "When we think of the 21st century, we think of technology: space, travel, biotechnology, robots. But the face of the future is more complex than the technology we use to envision it. The most exciting breakthroughs of the 21st century will occur not because of technology but because of an expanding concept of what it means to be human" (1990, p. 16).

Of the ten trends Naisbitt and Aburdene project, the first, a global economic boom, is the most relevant to this discourse. The emergence of free trade is a key reason for this, however, "the movement to global free trade is being driven by an alliance between telecommunications and economics" (1990, p. 23). They assert that just as manufacturing was the driving force in the industrial period, telecommunications, coupled with computers, will be the driving force for this current change. "We are laying the foundations for an international information highway system. In telecommunications we are moving to a single worldwide information network" (p.23). This will allow for all forms of communication, be it voice, data, text, or image, to be communicated instantaneously with anyone, anywhere (pp. 19–23).

A more theoretical view of the future is found in the book, *2020 Vision: Transform Your Business Today to Succeed in Tomorrow's Economy* written by Stan Davis and Bill Davidson in 1991. Davis and Davidson state that the information economy currently being experienced will last about seventy years and is, in fact, already half over. They view the life cycle of an economic phase in much the same terms as used to classify the cycles of a business or an industry. Applying slightly different labels to the traditional four phases results in the gestation, growth, maturity, and aging phase. This is analogous to human life. However, whereas the end of the human life cycle is death, the end of an economic life cycle is less ominous; it is merely the end of dominance. The information age is somewhere between the growth and maturity phase and is projected to remain dominant until around the year 2020, when another economic cycle is expected to emerge (pp. 14–24).

To capitalize on this information economy, realize that "information-based enhancements have become the main avenue to revitalize mature businesses and to transform them into new ones" (Davis & Davidson, 1991, p. 17). The word "informationalize" (p. 17) was coined to express this concept using information as a business strategy. When considering this instruction, one must bear in mind the technology itself is not the answer, but that, "businesses evolve from an amalgam of technological push and market pull" (p. 23) and that these must be kept in balance (pp. 17–23).

Building upon a distinction first made by Aristotle, the authors consider both the form and function of the architecture of information. Namely, that the forms of information are data, text, sound, and image. This matches the aforementioned list by Naisbitt and Aburdene (1990, p. 23). The corresponding functions of information are its generation, processing, storage, and transmission. Envision these two categories (form and function) graphed at right angles on a two-dimension graph. The result is sixteen distinct classifications. For example, the telephone began as the transmission of sound, whereas the computer was designed to process data. This resulting "information grid provides entrepreneurs and managers with a roadmap to the second half of the information economy" (Davis & Davidson, 1991, p. 31). Davis and Davidson state that "the blending of forms will be largely between data and text of computers and the sound and image of phone and television" and that "in the 2010s, phone, computers, and televisions may be virtually one and the same thing" (p. 34). The logical conclusion is that "the more [forms and functions] that you use, the greater your advantage" (p. 31) (Davis & Davidson, 1991, pp. 24–34).

"Different industries will figure out how to informationalize at different places, but just as they all industrialized, they will all eventually informationalize" (Davis & Davidson, 1991, p. 63). Although this truism applies to all industries, it does not necessarily imply that all businesses within the industry will successfully make that transformation. Davis and Davidson offer several equations which are expected to emerge in the second half of the information age and paint a picture of the future. Those relevant to the telephone answering service industry are as follows: "Informationalization = Customized Products + Rapid Response" (p. 63), "Information + Direct Access = Higher Service Standards" (p. 72), "Informationalization = Interorganizational Bonding" (p. 75), and "Informationalization + Logistics = Globalization" (p. 76).

Davis and Davidson use the example of a turbocharger (pp. 82–110), which runs off the exhaust, or by-product, of a car, and encourages business owners to "turbocharge information services" (p.82). There is tremendous opportunity in turbocharging information. An example would be TV Guide, essentially a listing of televisions shows, which was sold in 1987 for more than any of the three major networks it reported on. The Official Airlines Guide (OAG) is another such example; it too was sold for more than many of the major airlines whose schedules it communicated. In both cases this information was publicly available, but needed to be gathered, organized, and conveniently packaged (pp. 82–85). Add to this the warning that "when existing industry participants neglect the information dimensions of their business, for whatever reasons, independent third parties emerge to fill this role" (p. 96). While all businesses will informationalize in some fashion, it becomes a strategic choice as to how they do so. The authors apply a variation of the 80-20 rule to this situation saying, "that by 2020, 80 percent of business profits and market values will come from that part of the enterprise that is built around info-business" (p.108). They prophetically warn that "the dreamers always rush to put the vision into place, through merger and acquisition, within a couple of years. Few survive" (p. 109).

They quote Picasso as saying, "Every act of creation is first of all an act of destruction" (Davis & Davidson, 1991, p. 111). Continuing, they state, that "executives who accept the mortality of their own company are more likely to start bearing and nurturing new companies shortly after their own has reached adulthood," that is, the mature stage of the business cycle, (p. 120). These new creations will need to be "a real-time organization" (p. 117), "must be easy to use, friendly, seamless, and transparent" (p. 142), and be "flat, flexible, and built around teams" (p. 143).

Strategizing for the Future

Much has been written on the topic of developing business strategies. One such text, *The Strategy Process*, by Henry Mintzberg and James Brian Quinn (1991) provides valuable insight to the strategic process. Quinn defines strategy as "the pattern or plan that integrates an organization's major goals, policies, and action sequences into a cohesive whole, (p. 5). Mintzberg in turn says, "strategy is a plan—some sort of consciously intended course of action, a guideline (or set of guidelines) to deal with a situation" (p. 12).

When considering strategic development, first consider generic strategies. Generic strategies refer to common strategies which are typically followed in specific situations. Over the years various authors have proposed lists of these generic strategies. Mintzberg groups all these strategies into five categories: locating the core business (strategies relating to a business stage or industry), distinguishing the core business (looking within the business), elaborating the core business (considering how to enlarge or develop the business), extending the core business (by linking up with other businesses), and reconceiving (redefining) the core business (pp. 70 - 82).

Although generic strategies offer general guidelines and direction, Quinn states, that "the real strategy tends to evolve as internal decisions and external events flow together to create a new, widely shared consensus for action among key members of the top management team" (p. 96). Quinn then advocates a "logical incrementalism," which is a "conscious, purposeful, proactive, [and] good management," mode of operating (p. 104). Similarly, Mintzberg views an effective strategy as one which was crafted. Metaphorically, he views managers as craftsmen and strategy as clay. Contrary to popular belief, however, strategies are not necessarily a deliberate process, but can also be emergent, or more precisely a combination thereof (pp. 105–114).

In implementing a business strategy three organizational issues must be successfully addressed and handled. They are dealing with structure and systems, dealing with culture, and dealing with power (pp. 307, 351, 369). Failure to factor in and include these issues and their related complexity will make successful strategic implementation hard if not impossible.

In the same vein as generic strategies, there are also organizational contexts. "A context is a type of situation wherein can be found particular structures, power relationships, processes, competitive settings, and so on" (p. 601). The contexts Mintzberg and Quinn cover are the entrepreneurial context, the mature context, the diversified context, professional context, and the innovation context (pp. 601 - 602).

The entrepreneurial context (pp. 604–613) is the one most closely aligned with the typical telephone answering service. It features a simple structure, vesting power in the chief executive. There is little organizational hierarchy, and it is common for all employees to report to a single leader. In the entrepreneurial context, decision making is flexible and "handling disturbances and innovating ... are perhaps the most important aspects of the chief executive's work" (p. 605). Strategy decisions in an entrepreneurial organization rest with the chief executive. This obviously allows for centralization of the process, as well as flexibility and adaptability. Because the entrepreneur is also generally a visionary, it is much easier to implement a strategy within the entrepreneurial context.

One last aspect of the strategy process is managing change, since "to manage strategy is to manage change" (p. 759). Managing change is difficult, as most people view change as "a frightening situation." "Old rules no longer apply" and employees must develop "new skills and attitudes"; change "means moving from the familiar" to" a less-defined future" (p. 759). Failure to successfully manage the change will, undoubtedly, doom the strategy to failure as well.

Another business strategy text, *Strategic Management: Formulation, Implementation, and Control*, is also an excellent resource. Written by John Pearce and Richard Robinson, it outlines a logical and pragmatic process by which a strategy can be developed, deployed, and refined over time. "Strategic management is defined as the set of decisions and actions that result in the formulation and implementation of plans designed to achieve a company's objectives" (1997, p.3). The authors present a nine-step process for this all-encompassing approach.

The first step is to formulate the company's mission. The mission "is a statement, not of measurable targets but of attitude, outlook, and orientation" (Pearce & Robinson, 1997, p. 29). Beyond that, there is no hard, fast rule as to what should be included in a mission statement. Some common areas to consider are basic service, primary market, principle technology, goals on company survival, growth or profits, company philosophy, public image, and company self-concept. A good source for examples is the annual reports of companies, both in related and unrelated industries (pp. 29–51).

The next step is to take an internal look and develop a company profile. It will consider "the quantity and quality of the company's financial, human, and physical resources. It also assesses the strengths and weaknesses of the company's management and organizational structure" (p. 14). "A strength is a resource, skill or other advantage ... it is a distinctive competence" (p. 171). Conversely, "a weakness is limitation or deficiency in resource, skills or capabilities that seriously impedes a firm's effective performance" (p. 171).

Then consider the external conditions. These consist of opportunities for, threats to, and constraints upon the organization. These factors are divided into three classifications. The first is remote environment; it is the "economic, social, political technological, and ecological factors." The second is the industrial environment, which includes "barriers to entry, competitor rivalry, the availability of substitutes, and the bargaining power of buyers and supplies." The last category is the operating environment and includes the company's "competitive position, customer profiles, suppliers, creditors, and the labor market" (p. 96). Together the internal conditions and external environment can be determined via SWOT analysis. SWOT is an acronym which stands for strengths, weaknesses, opportunities, and threats (pp. 61–96).

Upon reviewing the SWOT analysis, several possible options will present themselves from which to choose. While the selection of the best option is a multifarious and, at times, an enigmatic effort, the key point is to make sure the option selected is relevant to and matches the company's internal resources and external environment (pp. 169–173).

Once the desired option has been selected, long-term objectives need to be developed to support it. "These are statements of the results a firm seeks to achieve over a specified period, typically five years" (p. 211). Planners generally place long-term objectives into seven classifications. These are profitability, productivity, competitive position, employee development, employee relations, technological leadership, and public responsibility (pp. 211–214).

Coincident to the determination of long-term objectives is the selection of a grand strategy. The purpose of a grand strategy is to "provide basic direction for action" (p. 218). These generic grand strategies run the gambit from growth to liquidation. In all fourteen grand strategies were listed. Concentrated growth, market development, product development, and innovation are typical and straight-forward strategies. The next group included horizontal integration, vertical integration, concentric diversification, and conglomerate diversification. The next three grand strategies deal with companies in crisis; they are turnaround, divestiture, and liquidation. Lastly are the corporate combinations, which are joint ventures, strategic alliances, and consortia (pp. 218 - 240).

Once the dual decisions of a grand strategy and long-term objectives have been determined, the next step is to determine annual goals and short-term objectives. To be effective, these short-term goals must be first linked to the long-term objectives and be measurable. Just as generic grand strategies were offered to complement long–term objectives, functional tactics are offered to provide focus and direction of annual goals for each functional unit of a company (pp. 304–308).

Implementing the strategic decisions is the next step in the strategic planning process. In this phase, "four fundamental elements must be managed to 'fit' a strategy if the strategy is to be effectively institutionalized: organizational structure, leadership, culture, and rewards, (p. 366).

Implementing the plan is not the end of the process, however. Next, it needs to be monitored and evaluated. To do so, control processes must be implemented. These controls are needed "to track the strategy as it is being implemented, to detect underlying problems, and to make necessary adjustments" (p. 397).

Writing for *Inc.* magazine, Donna Fenn's November 1997 article, "No More Business as Usual" states, "serious strategic planning forces you to change your company—and yourself" (p. 114). Fenn documents five self-analysis questions a business leader should consider before embarking on a strategic planning endeavor. First, is there a recognized need for change? If the need is not acknowledged, planning is in vain. Next, is there a willingness to accept honest feedback, no matter how painful? A plan that addresses only nonvolatile issues will be incomplete and unsuccessful. Thirdly, is there an earnestness to actually change the business? Without this vital quality, change will not occur. Next, will the plan be turned into action? A plan without follow-through is little different than no plan at all. And lastly, will the company's leaders have the courage to pursue the unknown and the untried? Without this bravado the most potentially rewarding parts of the plan will never bear fruit (pp. 114, 119).

The article's sidebar included the strategic planning steps recommended by Ron Myers, an American Management Association instructor. These seven steps closely follow those covered by Pearce et al. although they are less academic and more pragmatic. They are: (1) "develop a statement of purpose," (2) "conduct a SWOT analysis," (3) "compose a vision statement," (4) "state objectives," (5) "devise strategies for each objective," (6) "create action plans for each strategy," and (7) "draft a follow-up schedule" (Fenn, 1997, p. 114).

<u>Conclusion</u>

Although there is little in the way of scholarly works relating directly to telephone answering services, there is a vast array of informal writings, as well as relevant and insightful related information. This lengthy literature review began with insider views, moved on to perspectives from the larger telecommunications arena, and concluded with academic books and writings of a general business nature, but with applications to this particular focus of investigation. In total, these sources offer ample illumination and thoughtful provocation to suggest multiple answers to the singular question of what the future holds for the telephone answering service industry.

The key options are shown below in Figure 1.

- Growth via acquisition to achieve economies of scale.

- Position business to be acquired.

- Develop a market niche.

- Diversify into the call center industry.

- Increase rates.

- Go public.

- Improve sales and marketing efforts.

- Diversify into related industries.

- Pursue internet opportunities.

- Develop a formal strategic plan.

- Perform a SWOT analysis (Strengths, Weaknesses, Opportunities, and Threats).

Figure 1: <u>Key Options from Literature Search.</u>

CHAPTER 3: METHODOLOGY

Introduction

The literature review looked at several general business references about strategic planning. One aspect of strategic planning is performing a SWOT analysis. SWOT is an acronym for Strengths Weaknesses, Opportunities, and Threats, where strengths and weaknesses are an internal look at a business while opportunities and weaknesses are an external look at the surrounding business environment. Unfortunately, the literature review of industry literature revealed very little information which related to or could be used to infer an accurate and complete SWOT analysis. Therefore, additional information needed to be gathered from within the industry, in order that a cohesive and complete SWOT analysis could be completed.

Research Method

A simple survey was designed to obtain input from those in the industry to compile industry strengths, weaknesses, opportunities, and threats. The survey needed to be short enough to not discourage potential participants from completing it yet detailed enough to procure the requisite detail and depth. To achieve brevity, it was limited in the number of questions relating to the research topic. Some optional profile questions were added at the end to compile demographic information about each participant. To achieve the goal of depth and diversity, the response format was open-ended, short answer. An open-ended format allows participants to provide as much or as little feedback as they feel is appropriate for each question. It also is the answer format least likely to interject the opinions and preconceived ideas of the survey designer.

Survey Dissemination and Retrieval Method

There are several methods by which a survey can be conducted. The most common survey method is via telephone. Other options, in order of frequency of use, include mail, in-person, fax, and email. Phone surveys are expensive and time-consuming to conduct but do offer interaction to occur between the questioner and the person being surveyed; they also have a good response rate. In the same manner, in-person surveys offer interaction to occur as well as a high response rate but are the most time-consuming and expensive of all methods. They also are not practical for diversely located groups, as in this case. Mail is another option, but which still bears a moderate expense, is slow, and suffers from a low response rate. Using facsimile as a distribution method is less costly and much faster. Its chief limitation is that only those with access to fax machines can be surveyed. Lastly is email, the most recent alternative for conducting surveys. Email surveys have virtually no cost to conduct and take very little time to do. Again, they are limited to those who have access to and use email.

If the purpose of this survey was to get a good cross section response from the industry, then a telephone or mail survey would provide the best results. Surprisingly, surveying a good cross section to get an average or composite response was not the goal. Rather, the goal was to tap those in the industry who are innovators and leaders, those who can provide valuable insight and thought-provoking ideas. It makes no sense to develop a vision for the future based on input from those who conduct their business in isolation and operate on a day-to-day basis; these businesses may not even be around in five years, so why follow their lead? With this in mind, email was chosen as the dissemination and retrieval medium of choice for the survey. It was accepted, by the survey designer, that a large portion (but certainly not all) of those who were sought after to complete the survey have and use email. Conversely, it is accepted that a significant percentage of those whose input was not sought, do not have email. Naturally there are exceptions to both positions, however, email should effectively zero in on many of the desired participants.

Survey Procedure

Within the industry, there exists several email lists. An email list is, as the name implies, a compilation of email addresses. Those on the list subscribe to the service and have a common point of interest. To send a message to the entire list, simply send an email message to a special "list" address. Email sent to this special address will be received at the mail list's computer, which will in turn resend it to everyone on the list. This process generally only takes a few minutes, regardless of where the original sender or the end recipients are located. Also, email lists can either be "open" or "closed." An open list will allow anyone to subscribe to it and to do so without restriction. Conversely, a closed list is limited to those who comprise a certain group or who have certain qualifications; their subscription request must be approved before being added to the mail list.

It was decided to utilize three closed industry email lists for the purposes of the survey. The author of this thesis is a subscriber on all three lists (which was essential since the lists are closed). It should be noted that other email lists also exist within the industry but were not used. A message was posted once to each list seeking parties interested in taking part in industry research to be used in completion of a master's thesis. The text of this initial email is contained in figure 2 below. The complete email messages are contained in Appendix D.

"Hi, I am currently writing my master's thesis which is about the future of our industry. For part of my research, I would gratefully appreciate your input. If you would be interested in answering a 5-question questionnaire, please let me know by emailing me directly at: dehaan@xxxxxx.com. For those participants who are interested in the results of the research, I will make available a confidential and generic summary (that is, all identities will be protected). (This message is being posted to three mail lists; I apologize if you got it multiple times.) Thank you for your assistance."

Figure 2: <u>Text of Email Message Soliciting Survey Participation.</u>

Those parties who were interested in completing the survey sent a personal email back to the researcher requesting a survey. The researcher responded by sending the survey, again using email. The survey itself was not sent to the email list, but privately to each interested participant. The survey gave instructions on how to complete it and to email it back upon completion. No deadline was given, however, for the group who requested the survey but failed to return it, a second survey was sent via email, reminding them of their interest and setting a one-week deadline for completion.

Survey Design

The survey consisted of five questions relating to the research topic and three optional demographic profile questions for additional analysis. The first four of the five questions directly followed the SWOT analysis procedure previously described. They were as follows:

1. "In general, what do you think are the strengths of bureaus in the TAS industry?"

2. "In general, what do you think are the weaknesses of bureaus in the TAS industry?"

3. "What do you think are the current opportunities for bureaus in the TAS industry?"

4. "What do you think are current threats to bureaus in the TAS industry?"

The fifth question solicited conclusions from the participants as to how to integrate their responses into a plan for the future. That question was, "In light of your answers, what would you recommend a bureau in the TAS industry do to prepare for the future?"

In all five questions, the focus was on the industry as a whole as opposed to the respondent's own business. This was purposefully done to not only solicit a more generic response, but also to not put respondents in the awkward position of divulging information and ideas which they would be reluctant to share, might consider a competitive advantage, or could be deemed proprietary.

In order to assure a common perspective among the surveyed,

when answering the questions, definitions were included so that all participants would have a common frame of reference. The definitions were are follows: "A strength is a resource, skill, or other advantage relative to competitive alternatives," "a weakness is a limitation or deficiency in resource, skills, or capabilities that seriously impede an industry's effective performance," "an opportunity is a major favorable situation in an industry's environment," and "a threat is a major unfavorable situation in an industry's environment." An additional benefit of including definitions was that the definitions could provide a general direction towards areas for participants to consider and evaluate for inclusion in their responses. So that the biases of the survey designer would be minimized, the definitions were derived from Pearce and Robinson's *Strategic Management* (1997, p. 171). Whereas Pearce and Robinson's definitions were directed at an individual business, the definitions were adapted in the survey to reflect the industry as a whole.

Three profile questions were also included for possible breakdown analysis of the returned forms. These three questions were included at the discretion of the survey designer as it was thought survey responses may vary based on the vocational position of the respondent, tenure in the industry, or possibly age. The questions were, "your title," "number of years in the TAS industry," and "your age group." For the later question, six categories were presented. They were, "under 18," "18 to 24," "25 to 32," "33 to 51," "52 to 65," and "66 and above." These age ranges were included to categorize responders based on typical age demographic classifications. The category, "under 18" would represent a "pre-adult" demographic, born after 1980, which were not expected to be part of the surveyed group. The next grouping, "18 to 25" would be the oft mentioned and greatly misunderstood "generation X" or "gen X" classification. These individuals would be born between 1973 and 1979. The third range, "25 to 32" would be the "baby bust generation," born from 1965 to 1972. The "baby boomers" were the next classification. They would be ages 33 to 51, born between 1946 and 1964 (post World War II). Next, was ages 52 to 65, the "preretirement" category, born 1932 to 1945. Last, but not least, was the over 66 group, born prior to 1931, making up the "retirement age" demographic. Because individuals are greatly influenced by the events that occur in their teen and young adult years (Berkowitz et al., 1997, p. 80), it may be instructive to determine if any significant variances in answers or perspectives occur based on age group.

After the profile information, a final follow-up question was asked, "Do you want to receive a summary of the results of this survey?" This was done as an inducement and incentive to complete and return the survey, as well as to reward the efforts of those completing the survey, offering something of value in return for their time and labor.

The survey also contained instructions. It began with an introduction, followed by the opening instructions, which read, "Thank you very much for your willingness to assist with my thesis research. Instructions: Please read the definitions at the end of this message, click on 'reply,' and answer the following five questions, along with the profile which follows."

The survey concluded with, "Your willingness to answer this questionnaire and assist with this research is greatly appreciated. Again, thank you." The aforementioned definitions appeared at the very end of the survey.

Analysis of the Survey

Surveys were returned via email. To be easily read and answered by the largest possible group, all the communication was done it a straight text format. Because of this, and the fact that the questions were open-ended, it was not possible to directly import returned surveys into a database. Sadly, this was a manual process.

The surveys were printed and the answers to each question were examined to determine generic response categories. Once the general response categories were determined, the answers were coded, as were the first two profile questions, which referred to position and tenure in the industry (age was already coded by group). The coded responses were entered into Microsoft Access, a relational database. One survey was entered per record. Also entered with each record was the email address of the respondent, for identification purposes, and the mail list(s) which the respondent subscribed to.

The computer used for this was a standard personal computer, a Toshiba Tecra, model 510 CDT; aside from extra RAM (which was not needed for this application), it was not changed in any way from the factory configuration. This was the same computer used to send and receive the email surveys, as well as to write this thesis.

Limitations of the Research Survey

As with any research survey, there are inherent, unavoidable limitations. First and foremost are the biases and preconceptions of the researcher/survey designer. The researcher decided which literature sources to consult and chose what to report on from the literature search and review. It was this literature search which provided the basis for the questions comprising the survey. Since the researcher wishes to apply answers and conclusions from this research effort to an individual situation, there was every reason and incentive to remove all known personal propensities and prejudices for fear of impacting, and thereby tainting the results. Still, it is likely that particular leanings may remain which will skew the results or that there are personal inclinations which are unknown to the researcher and could not, therefore, be screened out. Also, the coding of the data was a subjective matter and not without misinterpretation. Additionally, the researcher's own education and tenure in the industry may have introduced a biased perspective or could have resulted in a tendency to gravitate towards the industry's conventional wisdom. Taken together, the researcher himself may be the biggest limitation to the survey, and this thesis, regardless of the steps taken to eliminate it.

Another limitation is the authors of the literature sources which were studied. For the most part, they were offering their opinions which were subjective and were not objective, containing provable and undisputed facts. Their opinions are just that, based either on empirical information, subjective conclusions, or even containing hidden agendas. There is no suggestion that the literature included contains such leanings, but it is wise to consider that they could exist. As mentioned above, it was the results of the information obtained from the literature search which first showed that a survey would be warranted and later formed the basis for the contents of the survey.

The most unknown limitation is with the group targeted for the survey. Was it legitimate to consciously direct the survey to specific groups within the industry? Was it constructive to purposely shy away from those deemed (by the researcher) not likely to have noteworthy, relevant, or significant input? Was email the proper medium to use for the dissemination and retrieval of the survey? The answers to these questions need to be carefully weighted by those who wish to use, consider, and apply the results.

The final limitation comes from those who completed the survey. Just as the researcher has biases and preconceptions, so do the respondents. Just as the possibility that a hidden agenda could exist among the literature authors, so to among the respondents. Again, do not infer that this is the case. Collectively, there was an overwhelming degree of support for the researcher's efforts and great interest in the results of the survey from those who chose to participate.

Conclusion

While every effort was made to obtain as much valuable and reliable information from as many sources as possible and to analyze said data in an unbiased and scientific manner, it is wise to consider the ways in which the results could lack objectivity. The methodology of the data gathering and processing procedure was documented so that it could be scrutinized by those who wish to consider and apply the results of this effort. Those who elect to do the latter should carefully consider the former.

CHAPTER 4: DATA ANALYSIS

Introduction

This chapter deals with the analysis of the data. First, the survey itself will be covered. Next, the participant's profile will be summarized and examined. Lastly, the responses to the survey will be covered and analyzed.

The survey itself concludes by directly offering recommendations. However, all aspects of the survey represent implied recommendations for consideration.

Survey Overview

As previously mentioned, all communications relating to the survey was conducted using email. The survey was sent out, via email, to industry members who had positively responded to an earlier request for participation in the survey. This request for participation was emailed, one time only, on October 23rd, 1997 to three industry mail lists. As interested parties responded affirmatively that they wished to complete the survey, the survey itself was emailed to them. The first interested party responded within hours of their initial request for participation on October 23rd. Additional affirmative responses trickled in over the next week and a few into the month of November. The final willing participant responded one month later on November 23rd, 1997. Altogether, forty individuals expressed interest in completing the survey.

Completed surveys began arriving on October 24th, 1997. This attests to the rapid feedback possible using email, which was one reason for selecting it as a transmission medium. By December 10th, 1997, a total of twenty-three completed surveys had been returned, along with one refusal.

This left sixteen of those originally expressing interest who did not, for one reason or another, complete their survey. For these sixteen, a second survey was sent out on December 15th, 1997. This time a deadline for completion was included; it was December 20th, 1997 at 8:00 a.m. Eastern Standard Time. Of this group of sixteen, five more responded, returning their completed surveys between December 15th and 19th, 1997.

In total, twenty-eight completed surveys were returned. A summary of this survey email activity is in Table 1.

Table 1: <u>Summary of Survey Email Activity</u>

<u>Date(s)</u>	<u>Activity</u>
Oct. 23rd	Posted requests seeking survey participants.
Oct. 23rd–Nov. 23rd	Received 40 requests to participate.
Oct. 23rd–Nov. 23rd	Sent out 40 surveys as they were requested.
Oct. 24th–Dec. 10th	Received 23 completed surveys; one refusal.
Dec. 15th	Sent survey second time to the remaining 16 individuals.
Dec. 15th–19th	Received 5 additional completed surveys.

Analysis of Participants

The initial request for survey participants was sent to three industry email lists. Each list was sponsored by an industry group and closed to those outside their respective organization. The first list was sponsored by ATSI (Association of Telemessaging Systems International, Inc.). At the time the message was posted, the list contained 146 names. Four names were duplicated, leaving 142 names unique to that list. The second list was sponsored by NAEO (National Amtelco Equipment Owners), an equipment user group. At the time of the original post, this list contained fifty-seven names, fifty-six of which were unique to the list. The final list was sponsored by PIN (Professional Inbound Network), a software user group. At that time, the PIN list contained sixty-nine names; all names sixty-nine names were unique to that list. (Refer to Table 2.)

Table 2: Analysis of Lists

List Name	Total Names	Unique Names
ATSI	146	142
NAEO	57	56
PIN	69	69
Totals	272	267
Less Duplicate		-26
Adjusted Total		241

Somewhat complicating matters was the fact that several individuals were included on more than one list. Eleven people subscribed to both the ATSI and NAEO lists; twelve to both ATSI and PIN; one to both NAEO and PIN; only the author was on all three lists. By subtracting those names who appeared multiple times, a total of 241 unique names appeared on the combined rosters, as shown in Table 2. (The details of this calculation is not as straight-forward as it would seem and is included in Appendix G for those so interested.)

As previously covered, a total of forty individuals expressed interest in completing the survey. When compared to the 241 unique names on the three lists, this is a seventeen percent survey interest rate (Table 3). Since only twenty-eight surveys were returned, this calculates to be a twelve percent response rate of the total population solicited and seventy percent of those initially expressing interest (Table 3).

Of the forty individuals who received the survey, seventy percent were from the ATSI list; twenty-eight percent form NAEO; and fifteen percent from PIN; see Table 4. (The percentages exceed 100 because of those individuals represented on two lists.) This indicates that the majority of those expressing interest in completing the survey were from the ATSI mail list and a minority from both NAEO and PIN.

Table 3: <u>Survey Interest and Completion Rates</u>

Category	Number	Percentage
Total Unique Names	241	100%
Requested Survey	40	17%
Completed Survey	28	12%

Table 4: <u>Breakdown of Surveys Requested</u>

List Name	Number of Requests	Percentage of Requests
ATSI	28	70%
NAEO	11	28%
<u>PIN</u>	<u>6</u>	<u>15%</u>
Totals	40*	113%*

* Actual totals (adjusted for names on multiple lists)

The percentages of those completing and returning the surveys, compared to the size of the mail lists are: ATSI, twenty percent; NAEO, twenty percent; and PIN, nine percent. Here it can be seen that one fifth of both the ATSI and NAEO lists actually completed and returned the survey, whereas a significantly smaller percentage did so for the PIN list, indicating less interest in participating (Table 5).

Table 5: <u>Analysis of Surveys Requested</u>

List Name	Number of Names	Requests	Percentage
ATSI	142	28	20%
NAEO	56	11	20%
PIN	69	6	9%

In considering the twenty-eight surveys that were completed and returned, a high percentage were from the ATSI list. ATSI represented sixty-eight percent of the returned surveys (nineteen out of twenty-eight). NAEO and PIN again represented minority input with twenty-nine (eight of twenty-eight) and eighteen (five of twenty-eight) percent respectively (see Table 6). This indicates that a majority of survey input came from those on the ATSI mail list. As such, the results of the survey will be skewed to reflect the membership of ATSI in general and the smaller ATSI mail list in particular.

Table 6: Breakdown of Surveys Returned

List Name	Number Returned	Percentage of Returned
ATSI	19	68%
NAEO	8	29%
PIN	5	18%
Totals	28*	100%*

* Actual totals (adjusted for names on multiple lists)

More telling, however, is the ratio of those completing the survey compared to those requesting it. ATSI had a sixty-eight percent completion rate (nineteen out of twenty-eight); NAEO had a seventy-three percent completion rate (eight out of eleven); and PIN had the highest completion rate at eighty-three percent (five out of six). These are shown in Table 7.

Table 7: <u>Analysis of Surveys Returned</u>

List Name	Requested	Returned	Percentage
ATSI	28	19	68%
NAEO	11	8	73%
<u>PIN</u>	<u>6</u>	<u>5</u>	<u>83%</u>
Totals	40	28	70%

The last group of statistics to consider regarding the make-up of the survey participants is the ratios of completed surveys compared to the total number of unique names on each list. A surprise emerges in this comparison, with the NAEO list having the highest participation rate at fourteen percent of all list members. ATSI is a close second at thirteen percent, with PIN a distant third at seven percent (Table 8). This is seen as an indication of interest in the research and the results, with NAEO and ATSI members having greater interest, in general, than PIN members.

Table 8: <u>Summary of Survey Participation</u>

List Name	Total Names	Completed Surveys	Percentage
ATSI	142	19	13%
NAEO	56	8	14%
PIN	69	5	7%
Totals	241*	28*	12%*

* Actual totals (adjusted for names on multiple lists)

The survey participants were asked to answer three profile questions. The purpose of this was to analyze survey answers by sub-category, however, there was not enough participation to make such analysis significant or meaningful. Nevertheless, the answers to these profile questions do provide some good insight into the overall makeup of the survey participants.

The first profile question was the title of the respondent. Seventy-five percent (twenty-one out of twenty-eight) were in upper management, having titles such as Owner, President, Chairman, and C.E.O. The next category was middle management, with eighteen percent (five of twenty-eight). One response came from an employee of an industry association, labeled as "other," and one survey did not respond to the question. The details of this profile question are shown in Table 9.

Table 9: <u>Title/Position of Survey Participants</u>

Title/Position	Number	Percentage
Upper Management	21	75%
Middle Management	5	18%
Other	1	4%
No response	1	4%

The next profile question asked the number of years the respondent had been in the industry. Two respondents did not answer this question. Of the remaining twenty-six, the longest tenure was thirty years and the shortest was two years. The average was 13.6 years of experience. (Collectively, the group represented 354 years of experience.)

Table 10: <u>Age Demographics of Survey Participants</u>

Age Group	Number	Percentage
25 to 32 years of age	3	11%
33 to 51 years of age	15	54%
52 to 64 years of age	9	32%
65 years and older	1	4%

The final profile question was the age group of the participants. A total of four age groups were indicated by the respondents, with the largest being the baby boomers representing fifty-four percent, a slight majority of all participants (refer to Table 10). As previously mentioned, individuals are influenced by their stage in the life cycle and by events which occur in their teens and early adult years. Therefore, it should be considered that the responses may be skewed toward the perspectives of the baby boom generation.

It is interesting to note that twenty-seven of the twenty-eight respondents requested that the results of the survey be forwarded to them. This implies that the opportunity to view the results was a motivating factor in survey participation. Also, a review of the email addresses of the participants revealed that twenty-five, or eighty-nine percent could be classified as owners or operators of telephone answering services, while the remaining three, or eleven percent could be classified as being in some sort of industry support role.

Overview of Analysis

As previously mentioned, the survey consisted of five open-ended questions to which twenty-eight individuals responded. The first four questions asked participants to describe the strengths, weaknesses, opportunities, and threats of the TAS industry, respectively. The final question asked for recommendations based on the aforementioned answers in questions one through four.

Virtually all participants gave multiple part responses to each of the five questions. Each response was identified and tracked separately. For the section on strengths, there was a total of seventy responses; weaknesses yielded seventy-nine; opportunities, eighty-five; threats, seventy-four; and recommendations an outstanding ninety-six. This is summarized in Table 11. Altogether, there were 404 responses on the twenty-eight surveys, which calculates out to over fourteen responses per survey. This is evidence of the effort and time that participants put into completing the survey.

Table 11: Summary of Survey Responses

Question	Total Responses	Responses per Survey
1. Strengths	70	2.5
2. Weaknesses	79	2.8
3. Opportunities	85	3.0
4. Threats	74	2.6
5. Recommendations	96	3.4
Totals	404	14.4

The responses from the first four questions have been classified as being optimistic/positive (answers to the strengths and opportunities questions) or pessimistic/negative (answers to the weaknesses and threats questions). The positive responses slightly outpaced the negative responses by a 155 to 153 margin. This indicates that, as a group, the answers from the participants were neither overly optimistic nor pessimistic but represented a well-considered and balanced view of industry conditions. On an individual level, however, some minor imbalances did occur. Four of the twenty-eight surveys were deemed as overly pessimistic because they had twice as many negative responses as positive. Correspondingly, one survey was judged to be overly optimistic because it had twice as many positive answers as negative. (Regardless of this optimistic and pessimistic labeling, all responses were included in the analysis.) The remaining twenty-three surveys were all nicely balanced between positive and negative answers.

Compilation of Findings

The first question of the survey was, "In general, what do you think are the strengths of bureaus in the TAS industry?" In response to this question, the twenty-eight respondents gave a total of seventy answers.

Leading all responses, representing half of the surveys and twenty percent of all answers, was the industry's flexibility to meet client needs. Adjectives such as adaptable, agile, innovative, personalized, and customized were used to express this sentiment.

Following at a close second in the strength category was the telephone staff or "live" person as it was frequently referred to. Included were comments about staff dedication and their training. Forty-six percent of surveys and nineteen percent of all answers reflected this thought.

Ranking third as a strength was technology, including the use of technology, investment in technology, and understanding of technology. These comments were directed at both computer technology and telecommunications technology. These references to technology were mentioned in thirty-nine percent of the surveys and comprised sixteen percent of the total answers.

The next strength was customer focus. This meant superior customer service, responsiveness to clients, attention to detail, and being people [client] oriented. This was for twenty-five percent of the surveys and ten percent of all answers.

Rounding out the top five strengths was being available twenty-four hours a day, seven days a week. This concept can be represented by the shorthand notation of "24 x 7." A summary compilation of all answers with multiple representations is shown in Table 12. The details of all responses are in Appendix H.

Table 12: <u>Summary of Strengths</u>

Category	Number of Answers	Percent of Participants	Percent of Total Answers
Flexibility	14	50%	20%
Staff ("Live" service)	13	46%	19%
Technology	11	39%	16%
Customer Focused	7	25%	10%
24 x 7 Staffing	5	18%	7%
Established business	3	11%	4%
Multiple niches to serve	2	7%	3%
Solution oriented	2	7%	3%
Can manage entry-level staff	2	7%	3%
<u>Other</u>	<u>11</u>	<u>na</u>	<u>16%</u>
Totals	70	na	100%*

* Adjusted for rounding

The second survey question was, "In general, what do you think are the weaknesses of bureaus in the TAS industry?" For this question, the twenty-eight surveys contained a total of seventy-nine responses. There were fewer unique responses to this question, but not as much overwhelming agreement on the top three answers.

The number one identified weakness related to low rates charged for services. Thirty-nine percent of all respondents and fourteen percent of all answers echoed this viewpoint.

Poor management skills were the second most often mentioned weakness, according to thirty-six percent of the respondents. This accounted for thirteen percent of all answers. Grouped into this category are problems and difficulties managing staff, lack of planning, poor financial planning, no succession planning, and poor growth management. Though these responses cover a wide array of issues, they are all easily summed up as management issues.

Poor marketing followed a close third, which was cited by thirty-two percent of the people and accounted for eleven percent of all answers. The marketing issues which were viewed as weak were a limited product mix, lack of self-promotion, lack of focus (trying to be all things to all clients), and lack of marketing knowledge. Also, criticized was an industry marketing perception that sales are a zero-sum game, that one service grows by taking a competitor's clients as opposed to finding new ones and adding them to the industry.

The fourth mentioned industry weakness was poor service. It was included in twenty-nine percent of the surveys and was mentioned ten percent of the time. Poor service was identified as abrupt staff, human errors, unprofessional, inconsistent, and not being flexible for the clients. A related issue, included here, is clients' expectations for immediate response in all aspects of the service, such as calls being answered on the first ring, no holds, and no delays on dispatching.

The fifth weakness was failure to keep up with technological changes. Twenty-one percent of the surveys made remarks about technology being a weakness; it was mentioned in eight percent of the answers. The technology issues were failure to keep up with technology, the cost of acquiring new technology, inability to fund research and development, resistance to technological change, and fear of new unproven technology.

These, as well as all answers with multiple responses are shown in Table 13. The details of industry weaknesses are covered in Appendix I.

Table 13: <u>Summary of Weaknesses</u>

. Category	Number of Answers	Percent of Participants	Percent of Total Answers
Low rates	11	39%	14%
Poor management skills	10	36%	13%
Poor marketing ability	9	32%	11%
Poor service	8	29%	10%
Technology	6	21%	8%
Low pay (wages)	5	18%	6%
Bad image	5	18%	6%
Entry-level employees	5	18%	6%
Competition from technology	4	14%	5%
Under capitalization	4	14%	5%
Labor intensive	4	14%	5%
Inadequate training	2	7%	3%
<u>Other</u>	<u>6</u>	<u>na</u>	<u>8%</u>
Totals	70	na	100%*

* Adjusted for rounding

The remaining three questions yielded responses which were more difficult to quantify and categorize. Unlike the answers to the questions on strengths and weaknesses, where each participant's multiple responses were distinct and non-overlapping, responses to the later three questions often resulted in a series of answers which were variations of the same theme or sequential suggestions following the same thread. In light of this outcome, the responses to the remaining three questions will be viewed only in terms of percentage of all answers and not also as percentage of all participants, as was done on the first two questions. Also, some interesting developments with the opportunities and threats questions will avail themselves to alternative evaluations as well.

The third survey question marked a transition to examining the external environment by asking the question, "What do you think are the current opportunities for bureaus in the TAS industry?" For this question there were eight-five responses, which were grouped into thirty-five categories. The clear leader among all responses was that technology provided the most significant opportunity for the TAS industry. Fifteen percent of all answers offered ways in which technology could be viewed as an opportunity. The increased availability and affordability of PC technology was mentioned as one such opportunity, as was using the features of the digital telephone network to better serve clients (which often requires a corresponding investment in computer technology for the telephone answering service). A subset of responses all proclaimed how technology could be used to get closer to clients and form tighter relationships. These observations included integrating with clients' databases and in-house computer systems, providing more reporting, and using technology for more effective and timely communications. The final technology issue was using remote stations, connected to the answering service system, for home-based TSRs and client-based locating of staff.

The next most mentioned opportunity was in providing telephone order-taking services. In fact, this is a primary focus of the PIN group, whose mail list was used as one of the survey groups. Yet it was not the PIN participants who made this suggestion, as they likely viewed this not as an opportunity but as a strength, since they had already capitalized upon it. Eleven percent of the responses mentioned telephone order-taking as an opportunity. By assuming that the five surveys completed by the PIN group (who already do telephone order-taking) would echo this sentiment, it is reasonable to argue that order-taking is in fact the biggest opportunity presented in the survey, at a projected sixteen percent of all responses. However, since this requires a bit of interpolation and, although logical, is presumptuous and unscientific, the suggestion of telephone order-taking as an opportunity will officially remain in second place at eleven percent.

The next opportunity envisioned was the internet. Seven percent of all answers made reference in one form or another to the internet. While some merely said "internet" others were more specific and mentioned the World Wide Web (WWW) or email. [It is not surprising that email would be mentioned since everyone completing the survey did so using email.] Also mentioned was the opportunity of integrating the internet (both the World Wide Web and email) into the answering service equipment.

Tied for the third most significant opportunity, at seven percent was niche markets. While some merely said that "niche markets" were an opportunity, others offered specifics, including personal service businesses, home offices, and the service industry, each receiving one mention.

Taking the opposite approach, with six percent of the vote, was the opportunity to become a one stop communication provider. This could include providing wireless communication (pagers, car phones, and PCS - personal communication services), internet access and services, long distance, etc.

These top five opportunities, along with all other responses receiving multiple mentions are included in Table 14; the complete list of responses can be found in Appendix J.

Table 14: <u>Summary of Opportunities</u>

. Category	Number of Answers	Percent of Participants
Technology	13	15%
Telephone order-taking	9	11%
Internet	6	7%
Niche markets	6	7%
One-stop shopping	5	6%
Geographic expansion	4	5%
Help desk service	4	5%
Consolidation	3	4%
Customer service lines	3	4%
Marketing	2	2%
Enhanced services	2	2%
Outsourcing	2	2%
Overflow calls	2	2%
Integration with voice mail	2	2%
"Live" service	2	2%
<u>Other</u>	<u>20</u>	<u>24%</u>
Totals	85	100%*

* Adjusted for rounding

Table 15: <u>Opportunities for New Services</u>

Category	Number of Answers	Percent of Participants
Telephone order-taking	9	11%
Internet	6	7%
Help desk service	4	5%
Customer service lines	3	4%
Enhanced services	2	2%
Outsourcing	2	2%
Overflow calls	2	2%
Integration with voice mail	2	2%
Selling ancillary services	1	1%
Appointment taking	1	1%
Health Care Services	1	1%
Information gathering	1	1%
Local peripheral services	1	1%
Selling local, long distance, calling cards	1	1%
Multi-tiered services to large clients	1	1%
Call center services to call centers	1	1%
Teleconferencing	1	1%
Telesales	1	1%

Of the thirty-five opportunities which were identified, eighteen of them, or fifty-one percent, fall into the singular classification of "new services." It is well to study and focus on this group of opportunities independent of distraction from the remaining forty-nine percent, which is in no way meant to detract from their own unique value. Shown above, in Table 15, is this list of new service opportunities.

Of this listing of eighteen possible new services, eight of them fall into a sub-grouping of "call center services." This is shown in Table 16. These services typically require additional equipment and software which the traditional telephone answering service does not possess. It also suggests that different paradigms must be adopted. Of all the opportunities suggested in the survey, new call center services were represented twenty-five percent of the time, indicating that this is a significant opportunity to pursue.

Rounding out the four SWOT questions was the other question looking at the external environment, "What do you think are the current threats for bureaus in the TAS industry?" The responses to this question numbered seventy-four and were grouped into twenty-eight different categories.

Table 16: <u>Call Center Services</u>

Category	Number of Answers	Percent of Participants
Telephone order-taking	9	11%
Help desk service	4	5%
Customer service lines	3	4%
Enhanced services	2	2%
Outsourcing	2	2%
Appointment taking	1	1%
Information gathering	1	1%
<u>Call center services to call centers</u>	1	<u>1%</u>
Totals	23	25%

The most often mentioned threat to the industry was competition from technology. It was given eleven times and accounted for fifteen percent of all answers. The sources of this competition were a vast array of technologies and services to track and worry about. The complete list of technological worries is shown in Figure 3.

- Internet [three mentions]

- Digital TV

- The [telephone companys'] intelligent network

- Wireless technology

- Voice mail

- Alpha-numeric paging

- Cellular

- Bypass technologies

- PCS (Personal Communication Services)

Figure 3: <u>Technological Competition.</u>

The second most frequently mentioned threat to the industry was labor concerns. This was cited eight times and represented eleven percent of all responses. The details are shown in Figure 4.

- Competition for existing labor pool

- Increased labor costs

- Unavailability of qualified applicants

- Maintaining a qualified workforce

- Labor issues

Figure 4: <u>Labor Concerns.</u>

The third threat was viewed as automation. It was cited five times in seven percent of all responses. Although much of what was included in the number one threat of competition could in fact be labeled as automation, the five responses included here simply listed automation and did not elaborate to tie it to a specific technology,

Also, listed five times was the threat of technology. This included new technology, incompatible technology, changes in technology, and changes in telecommunications, specifically.

A third item which was listed five times was unprofessionalism. Unfortunately, unprofessionalism is not actually a threat, but would more correctly be classed as a weakness. In fact, eleven of the twenty-eight categories of answers given to this question given were not external threats at all, but rather internal weaknesses. This presents a real problem in interpreting the data. One course of action would be to simply delete all answers which were not threats by definition, however this solution limits the scope of the answers to this question. Another scenario would be to remove the misdirected answers and insert them into the weakness category where they will belong, but this would skew the results for that question. A third option, and the one which will be followed, is to leave them here as reported by the survey respondents, since they represent the participants' perception of a threat. Indeed, based on these out-of-place answers, it could be argued that the industry's own weaknesses (as stated here) are a threat to itself; this could, in fact, have been the subconscious intent of the participants.

These top five answers, along with all other responses receiving multiple mentions are included in Table 17. The complete list of responses can be found in Appendix K; Appendix L subdivides these responses into true threats and actual weaknesses.

The capstone and concluding question was "In light of your answers, what would you recommend a bureau in the TAS industry do to prepare for the future?" There was the greatest number of responses to this question, totaling ninety-six answers. These were grouped into twenty-six recommendations.

The number one recommendation, cited in seventeen percent of the responses, was to acquire and use technology. Four individuals simply said to "computerize." Other noteworthy wording is shown in Figure

5.

Table 17: <u>Summary of Threats</u>

Category	Number of Answers	Percent of Participants
Competitive forces	11	15%
Labor pressures	8	11%
Automation	5	7%
Technology	5	7%
Unprofessional	5	7%
Complacent	4	5%
Call centers	3	4%
Negative public perception	3	4%
Undercapitalization	3	4%
Low pricing	3	4%
Weak management	3	4%
Other answering services	2	3%
Bad debt	2	3%
Decreased demand for service	2	3%
Lack of vision for the future	2	3%
<u>Other</u>	<u>13</u>	<u>17%</u>
Totals	24	100%*

* Adjusted for rounding

- Adapt emerging technologies to a people-oriented environment.

- Keep current with technology.

- Master equipment.

- Progressively invest in technology.

- Stay abreast of technology.

- Use new technologies.

- Telecommute.

- Use remote answering technology.

Figure 5: <u>Specific Technology Recommendations.</u>

The next most often mentioned recommendation was to improve staffing. This was included in fourteen percent of the responses. The essence of these comments could best be condensed into the admonition to hire and train quality people to consistently do their best and then compensate them accordingly.

These two recommendations were clear leaders among all recommendations. This is not surprising since both topics received considerable mention in each of the previous four questions.

The next five recommendations received only half as many mentions as the staffing advice. All five received seven mentions and accounted for seven percent of the answers. The first was to increase knowledge. Three respondents specified knowledge in the telephone network; two, knowledge in the industry; and two, knowledge in networking; Figure 6.

- Increase knowledge in the telephone network.

- Increase knowledge in the industry.

- Increase knowledge in networking.

Figure 6: <u>Recommendations to Increase Knowledge.</u>

Second, was to pursue a niche market. Specific examples suggested were medical, funeral homes, and alpha paging niches. One respondent said to identify one's current market and make that be the niche; Figure 7.

- Medical

- Funeral homes

- Alpha paging dispatch wholesale

- Make current business become a niche.

Figure 7: <u>Recommendations of Niches to Pursue.</u>

The next recommendation tied for third was to provide superior customer service. Phrases used in this group, include "be responsive to client needs," "enhance customer care," and "stay on top of client needs." Fourth of five, is the recommendation to diversify. The most often mentioned direction of diversification was into call center services, such as order taking. Also mentioned were enhanced messaging and fulfillment; Figure 8.

- Call center services

- Order-taking

- Enhanced messaging

- Fulfillment

Figure 8: <u>Options for Diversification.</u>

Rounding out the quintet of third place recommendations was the exhortation to increase profitability. A number of suggestions were offered on how this might best be accomplished, Figure 9.

- Price services right.

- Price services for profit.

- Take on higher margin accounts.

- Contain costs better.

- Reduce overhead.

- Reduce capital shortfalls.

Figure 9: <u>Recommendations On Increasing Profitability.</u>

These top seven recommendations, along with all other suggestions receiving more than one mention are shown in Table 18. The complete list is found in Appendix M.

Table 18: <u>Summary of Recommended Options</u>

Category	Number of Answers	Percent of Participants
Acquire and use technology	16	17%
Improve staffing	13	14%
Increase knowledge	7	7%
Pursue niche markets	7	7%
Provide superior customer service	7	7%
Diversify	7	7%
Increase profitability	7	7%
Grow middle management	5	5%
Achieve economies of scale via acquisitions	3	3%
Improve public relations	3	3%
Invest in marketing	3	3%
Develop a vision for the future	3	3%
Combine personalized service with technology	2	2%
<u>Other</u>	<u>13</u>	<u>14%</u>
Totals	24	100%*

* Adjusted for rounding

Significant Findings

The purpose of doing a SWOT (Strengths, Weaknesses, Opportunities, and Threats) analysis is to provide a springboard from which to suggest recommendations. The implication of the survey's SWOT observations is elegantly simple. Specifically, one must work to build upon strengths, shore up weaknesses, capitalize on opportunities, and counter threats. In light of this, the significant findings of the survey are not only the most frequently cited recommendations, but also the translations of the commonly mentioned strengths, weaknesses, opportunities, and threats into recommendations.

With this in mind, all categories of answers represented by ten percent or more of the responses were deemed to merit attention as being the survey's significant findings.

Quite simply, and without assumption, the significant recommendations directly from the survey are to acquire and use technology and to improve staffing. This is shown in Figure 10. Beyond that, attention must be given to the SWOT analysis to deduce additional recommendations.

- Acquire and use technology.

- Improve staffing.

Figure 10: Significant Direct Recommendations.

The significant strengths from the survey are flexibility, "live" service, technology, and customer focus. To translate these strengths into implied recommendations results in continuing to be flexible, to be customer focused, to capitalize on the availability of "live" staff twenty-four hours-a-day and reinforces the previously mentioned recommendation to acquire and use technology; Figure 11.

- Flexibility -> Strive for flexibility.

- Staff ("Live" service) -> Capitalize on 24-hour staffing.

- Technology -> Acquire and use technology.

- Customer focus -> Continue to be customer focused.

Figure 11: <u>Recommendations Implied by Significant Strengths.</u>

In like manner, the significant weaknesses identified in the survey are low rates, poor management skills, poor marketing ability, and poor service. Projecting these four weaknesses into recommendations advises one to increase rates, improve management skills, enhance marketing, and improve service: Figure 12.

- Low rates -> Increase rates.

- Poor management -> Improve management skills.

- Poor marketing ability -> Enhance marketing.

- Poor service -> Improve service.

Figure 12: <u>Recommendations Implied by Significant Weaknesses.</u>

The significant opportunities were identified as technology and telephone order-taking. Again, the implication is to acquire and use technology and also to diversify into telephone order-taking; Figure 13.

- Technology -> Acquire and use technology.

- Telephone order-taking -> Diversify into order-taking.

Figure 13: <u>Recommendations Implied by Significant Opportunities.</u>

The significant threats were characterized as competition from technology and labor pressures. The suggested recommendations to combat these threats would again be to acquire and use technology (so that it cannot be used against you) and also to develop a work environment which will be more attractive to prospective employees than other companies; see Figure 14.

- Technology competition -> Acquire and use technology.

- Labor pressures -> Increase employment attractiveness

Figure 14: <u>Recommendations Implied by Significant Threats.</u>

Of all these direct and implied recommendations, the significant recurring theme was technology. It appeared on all five lists and received more than ten percent response on four lists.

A summary of all significant recommendations, both direct and implied, is shown in Figure 15.

Direct Recommendations

- Acquire and use technology.

- Improve staffing.

Recommendations Implied from Strengths

- Strive for flexibility.

- Capitalize on 24-hour staffing.

- Acquire and use technology.

- Continue to be customer focused.

Recommendations Implied from Weaknesses

- Increase rates.

- Improve management skills.

- Enhance marketing.

- Enhance service.

Recommendations Implied from Opportunities

- Acquire and use technology.

- Diversify into order-taking.

Recommendations Implied from Threats

- Acquire and use technology.

- Increase employment attractiveness.

Figure 15: <u>Summary of Significant Survey Recommendations.</u>

Conclusion

The results from the surveys provide a wealth of information that offers several recommendations, both directly and indirectly, for the telephone answering service owner to consider in preparing for the future. These significant findings from the survey, along with the key options uncovered by the literature search, will be combined for analysis and consideration in Chapter 5.

CHAPTER 5: SUMMARY

Introduction

The overall intent of this research is to determine a recommended course of action for the Company, specifically, and telephone answering services, in general, to successfully prepare for the future. Chapter 2 summarized an extensive literature search which offered several viable alternatives for consideration. This input was gleaned from sources both within the industry and outside the industry. In the same manner and building upon the literature search, Chapter 4 likewise provided suggestions, both directly and indirectly, which can be added to the list for consideration and analysis.

Alternatives for Consideration

As mentioned above, Chapter 2 summarized the literature search. The chapter concluded with Figure 1, which shows the key options for consideration. These options, or alternatives, need to be analyzed and contemplated in order to make recommendations to prepare for the future.

Figure 1 is repeated below for reference.

- Growth via acquisition to achieve economies of scale.

- Position business to be acquired.

- Develop a market niche.

- Diversify into the call center industry.

- Increase rates.

- Go public.

- Improve sales and marketing efforts.

- Diversify into related industries.

- Pursue internet opportunities.

- Develop a formal strategic plan.

- Perform a SWOT analysis (Strengths, Weaknesses, Opportunities, and Threats).

Figure 1: <u>Key Options from Literature Search.</u>

Likewise, Figure 15, on page 147 in Chapter 4, presents a summary of options which resulted from the five survey questions. These options, which contain overlap and repeat themes from question to question, have been condensed to eliminate duplication and are summarized below in Figure 16.

- Acquire and use technology.

- Strive for flexibility.

- Capitalize on 24-hour staffing.

- Continue to be customer focused.

- Diversify into order-taking.

- Enhance marketing.

- Improve management skills.

- Enhance service.

- Enlighten staffing.

- Increase rates.

- Increase employment attractiveness.

Figure 16: Unique Survey Recommendations for Consideration.

Each list contains eleven items, for a total of twenty-two. Two items, however, are duplicates and appear on both lists. These two items are "increase rates" and "improve sales and marketing efforts." This leaves twenty individual items for analysis.

To further simplify the analysis, several of the alternatives listed are accepted as givens, that is, they are so basic and universally relevant to the industry that further analysis is not warranted; they should be pursued by all, regardless of any other alternatives which are deemed appropriate and implemented. They are flexibility, customer focus, improve management skills, enhance service, enlighten staffing, and increase employment attractiveness. These will be treated as a group, simply entitled "the basics."

These six items are listed in Figure 17.

- Strive for flexibility.

- Continue to be customer focused.

- Improve management skills.

- Enhance service.

- Enlighten staffing.

- Increase employment attractiveness.

Figure 17: <u>The Basics.</u>

By removing the two duplicates and separately grouping "the basics," the resulting list of alternatives to consider is pared down to fourteen items, Figure 18. Some of these are mutually exclusive, such as pursuing acquisition opportunities versus positioning to be acquired. Most, however, are not mutually exclusive and can therefore be used in tandem. The remaining fourteen alternatives for further considerations are summarized in Figure 18 and are listed in no significant order.

1. Growth via acquisition to achieve economies of scale.

2. Position business to be acquired.

3. Develop a market niche.

4. Diversify into the call center industry.

5. Increase rates.

6. Go public.

7. Improve sales and marketing efforts.

8. Diversify into related industries.

9. Pursue internet opportunities.

10. Develop a formal strategic plan.

11. Perform a SWOT analysis.

12. Acquire and use technology.

13. Capitalize on 24-hour staffing.

14. Diversify into order-taking.

Figure 18: <u>Key Alternatives for Consideration and Analysis.</u>

Analysis of the Alternatives

The relative merits of each of the fourteen alternatives must be carefully determined and weighed. This will allow the best combination of alternatives to be combined and integrated into a unified package of recommendations. Therefore, each of the fourteen alternatives will be considered and analyzed. It should be noted that the order of the alternatives is not significant but is rather in the order they have been presented throughout this work.

The first alternative is to seek "growth via acquisition to achieve economies of scale." This is a recurring theme in the literature search, mentioned by Michaels (1997c, pp. 1 & 6), Shatz (1996, p. 12), and others. It's also received attention in the survey as an opportunity which exists (five percent), as well as a survey recommendation to pursue (three percent). In neither case, however, were the mentions among the survey's leading responses. The wisdom of increasing efficiency by expanding the scope of operations, that is, scale, is well founded and a solid strategy (Orsino, 1994, p. 102). The warning to observe is to ensure effective management and control of the acquisition once it has been purchased (Orsino, pp. 122–127 and Church, 1995, p.8). The viability of this alternative is reduced to the availability of financing to complete the transaction and the depth and expertise of management to oversee it. If these are in place, this becomes a sound and viable strategy.

The next alternative is to "position business to be acquired." This did not appear at all in the survey responses, and in the literature search, it was implied more than anything. Quite simply, for every answering service that is bought by one company, an answering service is sold by another. As interest in making acquisitions increases, the demand will push up the value of profitable, desirable, well-run operations. This creates a real opportunity as an exit strategy for those wishing to leave the industry or retire.

"Developing a market niche" was an oft mentioned concept in both the literature search and especially the survey. It was mentioned as a strength, an opportunity, and a recommendation, with the latter two each at seven percent. Possible niches mentioned included medical (the competition for which was also viewed as a threat by three percent), funeral homes, alpha dispatch wholesale, small retail sales, personal business services, home office, and the service industry. (Interestingly, it was conversely mentioned that a weakness is being "a small, fragmented industry.") The merits of this alternative rest on the niche being considered, the size of the niche, and the existing knowledge the business managers have of the niche. This alternative of developing a niche market should be compared and contrasted to the antithetical alternatives of diversifying into the call center industry and into related industries.

The fourth alternative to be considered is to "diversify into the call center industry." This was advocated in the literature search by Osmon (1997, p.2), Shatz (1996, p.12) and others; it also received notable mention in the survey. As a survey recommendation, this alternative received a seven percent response. In the survey question on industry opportunity, call center services received widespread affirmation. Order-taking, which is the premier call center service, was mentioned eleven percent of the time. Other call center services seen as opportunities included help desks, customer service lines, enhanced services, outsourcing, appointment taking, information gathering, and providing niche services to other call centers. On the plus side of this alternative is the fact that the TAS industry already has experience with staffing and scheduling which are required in the call center environment (although it is often on a much larger scale). The downside from embarking on this route is that a call center (because of its larger size) requires more space than may be available for answering services and it necessitates a significant investment in technology. Both of these concerns have an associated expense which may limit some from considering it.

The fifth alternative is to "increase rates." This was one of two alternatives which are on both the list of key options from the literature search and the summary of significant recommendations from the survey. It is the number one stated weakness on the survey (fourteen percent), it received mention as a threat, and garnered a seven percent response as a recommendation. In the literature search, West (Michaels, C., 1997, p. 12), Osmon (1997, p.2), and many others implored industry members to increase rates. The wisdom of such advice seems self-evident. However, based on the number who decry the low rates charged by the industry, it would seem to be advice that should be carefully considered and followed. This alternative could arguably have been included in with the six basics already mentioned. However, it could be determined by some as a viable strategy to consider being a low-cost provider. This suggests that a premium or value pricing strategy is merely another business decision to make. It is important to note that many of the alternatives being considered carry a significant price tag; it will only be through profitable pricing that these other alternatives can be pursued.

The next alternative listed was that one to "go public." This was not mentioned at all in the survey responses, but was a theme explored in the literature search (Orsino, 1994, pp. 51–55 and Blowers et al, 1995, pp. 2–5). While the financial rewards to the business owner are quite high with a successful initial public offering, the stress and loss of control and privacy may be an overshadowing negative factor. Also, to be considered, is the feeling of Blowers et al (1995, p. 12) that a business should have at least twenty million in annual revenues and net earnings of at least one million before going public; that plateau puts this option out of reach for most telephone answering services. However, it may be an acceptable long-term goal, using some of the other alternatives to reach the twenty million mark.

Another seemingly self-evident alternative is to "improve sales and marketing efforts." This was the other alternative which was included on both the list of key options from the literature search and the summary of significant recommendations from the survey. Some sources, including Willis (Michaels, 1997, p. 1) discussed the importance of improving marketing and sales efforts. As far as the survey, it is the third biggest threat at eleven percent of all answers. Again, it can be argued that there are cases where better marketing is not warranted, needed, or desired in specific circumstances, however this is an unlikely situation. Just as in raising rates, increasing sales can be seen as a vehicle to finance some of the other alternatives.

The eighth alternative suggested is to "diversify into related industries." Emmett (1997, pp. 1–3), Page (1997, pp. 1–2), and others offered such diversification options as paging, cellular, alarms, office suites, voice mail, etc. Responses from the survey add various telecommunication services to the list. This alternative runs counter to the previously discussed alternative to develop a market niche, nevertheless, it is one to consider. On the plus side of any diversification is the fact that there is less exposure to the negative impact of market forces on an industry, since the scope of the business transcends any one industry (Orsino, 1994, p. 2). The downside of diversification, even into closely related industries, is getting away from core competencies and diluting financial and managerial resources. The end result could be doing many things poorly versus a few things well.

Next is the alternative to "pursue internet opportunities." Hastings, in the literature search (1996, p.12), saw the internet as an innovation to track and pursue. In the survey, the internet was the third ranked opportunity (it was also listed as a threat). It was not explicitly mentioned as a recommendation, though it is implied in the recommendation to acquire and use technology. The literature search also produced some compelling statistical projections of the future importance of the internet, both the World Wide Web and email. With Forrester Research (Cooperstein, 1997, p. 36) predicting that by the year 2001, email will have a fifty percent penetration rate, is this an opportunity which can be ignored? On the other hand, with the industry's claim to fame being its "live" staff, available twenty-four hours a day, will the technology of the internet serve to effectively disassemble this strength?

Strategic planning is not included directly among the survey responses, although there are the minority recommendations to be future focused and threats (weakness) from a lack of vision for the future, both at three percent. Strategic planning, however, did occupy much consideration in the literature search (Mintzberg & Quinn and Pearce & Robinson). Therefore, the alternative to "develop a formal strategic plan" is presented for consideration. The need to do so can be most eloquently summed up by the oft repeated saying, "Failing to plan, is planning to fail." Balancing that rhetoric, however, is the fact that most answering services are small businesses, run by entrepreneurs who plan as they go and are (usually) too busy for formal planning. However, it is critical to recall that developing a strategic plan is the purpose of this document. Therefore, the final recommendations soon to be made herein will form the basis of a strategic plan and as such it will be the basis for all recommendations.

The next alternative is to "perform a SWOT analysis." Indeed, that was exactly the design, intent, and purpose of the survey. Whereas the survey was a SWOT analysis of the industry, it needs to be made more personal and repeated at the business level. The survey itself can be easily adapted to individual businesses by altering language referring to the "industry" to indicate the "company." The results of each company's SWOT analysis can be compared and benchmarked with the industry results detailed in Chapter 4. The knowledge and insight gained will undoubtedly be invaluable. The only downside is the time to complete and compile the survey.

The consistent and prevailing theme of the survey answers, is best summed up by the admonition to "acquire and use technology." Conversely, very little of the literature search addressed this issue; though by implication, diversifying into the call center industry and pursuing order-taking business both require significant technology to accomplish. The only other reference to technology was Emmett's assertion that it should be used to reduce labor costs and could eliminate staffing altogether (1997b, p. 2). The general justification for technology investments, however, is to support the efforts of the

TSRs, allowing them to more effectively, efficiently, and intelligently interact with clients and their callers. The procurement of technology is a never-ending quest with no limit other than the means to finance it. The counter approach would be to avoid technology and make the investment totally in staffing. The problem with this approach is a shrinking labor pool and limited number of qualified candidates in most regions of the country. This suggests that more technology is needed to allow those qualified and competent employees who do exist to do their jobs as effectively as possible. In actuality, the question here is not one of rather or not to acquire and use technology, but of how much technology to acquire and use.

The next alternative to analyze is to "capitalize on 24-hour staffing." True, the twenty-four by seven staffing expectations of the industry's clients are a double-edged sword. It amplifies staffing and management challenges in an already labor-intensive industry. However, rather than fight this reality as Emmett would advocate, by eliminating labor through technology, the pragmatic solution is to not only accept it, but turn it into an asset and strength. Twenty-four by seven staffing is a barrier to entry and staffing liability which many potential competitors will not even consider; technology, on the other hand, can be bought and successfully implemented by almost any company, hence greatly reducing entry barriers.

The final alternative is to "diversify into order-taking." This is really a subset of the previously mentioned alternative to diversify into the call center industry. However, since order-taking is one the biggest call center services and one of the easier ones to learn (as opposed to help desks, appointment setting, customer service, outsourcing, etc.) it is presented separately as a possible stepping stone toward the bigger picture of the call center industry as a whole (although a call center could elect to do nothing but telephone order-taking). This is a tremendous opportunity as the market for call centers is several orders of magnitude greater than the traditional telephone answering service market. The areas of caution are an increase in scope, more staff to hire and manage, more equipment to install and maintain, more space needed, and higher client expectations. Most of these concerns, however, are common to any type of growth or expansion.

These fourteen alternatives and an overview of the analysis is included in Appendix N.

Recommendations

As previously mentioned, the list of the six basic alternatives are ones which transcend virtually all businesses and scenarios. As such they are, as a group, the first recommendation to follow.

Next are two more alternatives of universal benefit, namely doing a SWOT analysis and developing a strategic plan. These should be viewed as the foundation onto which the other recommendations can be built. Following this, for almost all businesses, the strategic plan will include three more recommendations of near universal appeal: increasing rates to ensure profitability and finance other recommendations, improving sales and marketing efforts, and capitalize on twenty-four-hour staffing. As a group, these should all be implemented in order to provide a strong base for the future and a strong support structure for the following remaining recommendations.

In reviewing the analysis of these remaining alternatives, it is apparent that several of the alternatives are not exclusive to each other and can be implemented in tandem. A few of the alternatives, however, are mutually exclusive or somewhat exclusive and preference must be given to one over the others. These will be reviewed first.

The second alternative, to position the business for acquisition, is a viable option for an owner wishing to exit the business, however, aside from this particular scenario, it is one inappropriate for any other circumstance. Similarly limited in practicality is the alternative of going public, since most services today do not have sufficient size to justify the attention required to anticipate a successful initial public offering. (However, as previously mentioned, this could be

156

adopted as a long-term goal, pending the successful completion of the recommendations which follow.) Because of their limited application, these two alternatives are rejected for future consideration.

The alternative to develop a market niche runs counter to the three alternatives of diversification (into a related industry, into order-taking, and into the call center industry). A market niche could undoubtedly be found which would be sufficiently large to justify focus. However, doing so would make the service even more vulnerable to threats the industry currently faces and which have previously been identified. It would seem logical, then, to pursue a diversification strategy. Diversifying into a related industry, such as alarms, paging, cellular, office suites, or secretarial service would somewhat build upon existing knowledge and experience, as well as benefit from the overlap of some clients. However, the risk exists of spreading oneself too thin and diluting both management and financial resources. This leaves diversification into order-taking and call centers as remaining preferable alternatives. Both of these options are paths in the same direction, only the distance to travel differs. While telephone order-taking could be the end all goal, it could also be a first step into the call center arena. The pragmatic approach would be to expand into order-taking and then re-evaluate the situation. At that point, a decision could be made rather or not to focus on order-taking or to move to embrace the greater call center industry.

The alternative to pursue internet opportunities could likewise be seen as a diversification strategy or viewed as complementing one's existing business. (The survey responses were ambiguous enough so as to be unsure of the scope of this alternative.) As a diversification strategy, pursuing the internet carries with it all the same concerns as seeking diversification into a related industry (which it is). As such this interpretation of the alternative is not recommended. However, pursuing internet opportunities to complement, support, and expand an existing business is an alternative which cannot be ignored and must be recommended.

Both the internet and order-taking recommendations will require investment in technology. By necessity, it too then is a requisite recommendation. It does not stop however with those two areas. Technology needs to be acquired and used in all facets of the business, wherever it can reduce operating costs, enhance service, or stay one step ahead of the competition.

An optional parallel recommendation is to pursue acquisition opportunities. Before proceeding, however, a careful internal evaluation must be conducted. First, determine if sufficient company infrastructure is in place to handle the problems resulting from integrating an acquisition. Then, acquisitions can be pursued as long as they make good business sense. That is, they must enhance the existing operation and not weaken it, they must fit into a logical expansion plan, and most importantly they must be for the right price. Given the uncertainty with the future of the traditional TAS industry it is not wise to make an acquisition which cannot be paid for in a few years. Also, guard against blindly pursuing an acquisition with unrealistic terms or conditions; know when to walk away. (See Figure 19, below.)

The basic six

- Strive for flexibility.

- Continue to be customer focused.

- Improve management skills.

- Enhance service.

- Enlighten staffing.

- Increase employment attractiveness.

The foundation

- Perform a SWOT analysis.

- Develop a strategic plan.

The near universal

- Increase rates.

- Improve sales and marketing efforts.

- Capitalize on twenty-four-hour staffing.

Major recommendations

- Diversify into telephone order-taking.

- Pursue internet opportunities.

- Invest in technology.

Alternate parallel recommendation

- Growth via acquisition

Figure 19: <u>Recommendations to Prepare for the Future.</u>

Conclusion

The telephone answering service industry has been explained, studied, surveyed, and analyzed. Recommendations have been made to allow it to prepare for the future. The next step is up to the reader to determine if the recommendations contained herein are reasonable and applicable to specific circumstances and then to react accordingly.

Appendix A: Summary of Industry History

Table 19: <u>Key developments in the Telephone Answering Service Industry</u>

<u>Approximate Year: Key Event</u>

1876: Bell invented the telephone.

1877: First basic telephone switching device

1880s: First long distance lines installed

1910: First transcontinental phone call

1917: First answering service: Kidd opens Doctor's Exchange Service" in Portland

1921: Boyton conceives "stop board."

1923: Freke-Hayes has PBX switch board modified for answering service, the forerunner to the "cord board."

1930s: Answering services sprout up around the country.

1930s to 60s: Cord boards and multi-button phones are common answering service equipment.

1950s: Curtin develops first line concentrator.

1968: Carterfone decision allows non-phone company devices to be connected to phone network.

1970s: Amtelco and others begin manufacturing replacements for cord board.

1980s: DID service and call-forwarding provide new options.

1983: IBM introduces PC.

1984: Forced divestiture of AT&T, providing impetus for rapid growth and innovation in telecommunications.

1983: Amtelco introduces second generation computerized systems; others follow.

1996: Telecommunications bill passed; deregulation of industry takes another giant step forward.

Appendix B: Definition of Terms

Definition of Terms

24 x 7: Call center shorthand to indicate continuous operations, twenty-four hours a day, seven days a week.

Agent: Another name for TSR.

Alphanumeric paging: One of four types of paging (the others being tone alert, voice, and numeric) which allows for a text message to be displayed on the pager. To send an alphanumeric page, a keyboard is required to enter the message and a modem is needed to access the paging system to send the information. Even with this limitation, alphanumeric paging is the fastest growing type of paging.

ANI (Automatic Number Identification): A telephone company service whereby the number of the calling party (and sometimes their name) is provided electronically to the called party while the phone is ringing. Special equipment is needed by the called party to read the ANI information.

Answering service: See, "telephone answering service."

Automated attendant: One type of voice mail service, which automatically answers a business line and plays a recorded list of numbered options for the caller to select so that their call might be properly routed. For example, press 1 for sales, press 2 for service, and so on.

BRI-ISDN (Basic rate interface ISDN): An entry level form of ISDN which allows for two main channels (for voice, fax, or data) and one data channel (primarily for control purposes); also call 2B+D. See, "ISDN."

Bureau: An alternate name for a telephone answering service.

Call center: A term generally applied to the telemarketing/order taking industry, it refers to the actual location where equipment and personnel are located to make and receive calls. In a generic sense a call center can also imply a telephone answering service, though in actual usage this is generally not the case.

Called party: The person being called (see, "calling party").

Caller: A customer or potential customer of a client of a telephone answering service or call center. The primary interaction of the staff of a telephone answering service is actually with the customers of their clients and not as much with the clients themselves.

Caller ID: A telephone company service whereby the number of the calling party (and sometimes their name) is provided electronically to the caller party while the phone is ringing. Special equipment is needed by the called party to read the caller ID information.

Call-forwarding: A telephone company service which will redirect a call from the called number to another number which has been selected by the called party. There are three common types of call-forwarding: basic call-forwarding (which is turned on and off by the user), call-forward when busy, and call-forward when there is no answer. Call-forwarding is the method generally used by a client to redirect their calls to their answering service.

Calling party: The person placing a call (see, "called party").

CAP (Competitive Access Provider): A telephone company which competes with the traditional local telephone company (who until recently was a protected monopoly). CAPs are thought to drive innovation and meet customer needs much better than the traditional telephone company. In virtually all cases CAPs serve to drive down prices for local phone service.

Case-based routing: Case-based routing is an expert systems technology which prompts the TSR to ask certain predefined questions, the answer to each question branches in a different direction to quickly and effectively handle the caller's needs. The benefits of case-based routing are shorter call times and the requirement for less training (St. Ledger, 1997, p. 3). See, "decision tree software."

Catalog/literature request lines: A segment of inbound telemarketing specifically to answer calls from those wishing to receive a catalog or brochure. This is generally in response to various types of advertising promotions.

Central office: A telephone company facility where the customers' lines are connected to switching equipment so that they can call other numbers, both locally and long distance.

Client: A customer of a telephone answering service or call center.

Concentrator: An essentially obsolete device, designed to replace cord boards, which was used as a termination point for off-premise extensions of an answering service's client's lines. The concentrator funnels calls to another piece of equipment so that they can be effectively answered.

Cord board: A obsolete device, and forerunner to the concentrator, which was used as a termination and answering point for off-premise extensions of an answering service's client's lines.

CTI (Computer-Telephony Integration): Completely interconnecting a computer system with a telephone switch to allow relevant computer database information about the caller or account to be presented to the TSR simultaneously with the call itself.

DID: An acronym for Direct-Inward-Dial; it refers to a telephone company provided service combining the flexibility of hundreds of numbers with the economy of significantly fewer discrete lines (trunks). Telephone answering services frequently use DID service as it allows for hundreds of clients to receive individual, personal service, without incurring the expense of maintaining a discrete connection for each client.

Dispatch: When a message is taken for a client, it must be somehow given to that client. This action is dispatching. Common dispatch methods include, (1) paging the client, (2) calling the client at a predetermined number, (3) holding the message for the client, (4) sending the message to a special desktop printer at the client's office, (5) sending the message to the client's fax machine, (6) recording the message for the client to retrieve at his convenience, and (7) sending the message to the client's email address. Sometimes multiple methods are used for redundancy and back-up purposes.

Dealer locator service: A segment of inbound telemarketing which allows callers to find relevant information about the store or location of a company nearest them. Typically, this is determined based on the caller's zip code, phone number, city, or state.

Decision tree software: A computer software program which asks a series of predetermined questions, each based on the answer to the previous question, allowing the user to reach a correct decision even though they do not personally have the expertise required to make such a decision. See, "help desk."

DNIS (Dialed Number Identification Service): For T-1 and DID service, a method of identifying each call by the called number. This allows TSRs to know the client each call is for and can be used to trigger a screen pop.

Errors and omission (E&O) Insurance: A special insurance policy to protect policy holders from the legal ramifications which could result from an error in handling a call or an act of omission for the same. Many telephone answering services and call centers carry this type of insurance to protect them from a potentially company-ending lawsuit in the unlikely event that a critical problem occurs.

Executive suites: An industry which provides basic office services to businesses or out-of-town companies. The basic provision includes an office, desk, and phone. Ancillary services might include copy and fax machines, receptionist and daytime answering service, conference facilities, and secretarial services.

First-level help desks: See, "help desk."

Help desks: Another segment of inbound telemarketing, whereby entry-level staff can use decision tree software to answer questions and provide basic support functions for technical applications. See, "decision tree software."

Inbound telemarketing: One of two aspects of telemarketing is where customers or prospects call a company for assistance when they want or need it as opposed to outbound telemarketing where the company calls customers or prospects. See, "outbound telemarketing."

Informationalize: The concept of using information as a business strategy (Davis & Davidson, 1991, p. 17).

Internet: An international network of networks, allowing email and information to be readily sent from one computer to another.

ISDN (Integrated Services Digital Network): An international standard for modern, all digital, telephony communications. There are two types of ISDN. See, "BRI-ISDN" and "PRI-ISDN."

IXC (Inter exchange carrier): A telephone company which does not provide local telephone service, but which provides some aspect of long-distance service. Traditional examples of IXCs are AT&T, MCI, Sprint, etc.

Literature request lines: See, "catalog request lines."

Live: A somewhat inane term to indicate that a call will be processed by a real person as opposed to automation from a voice mail system or an answering machine. The main benefit of a telephone answering service is that it provides "live" interaction with the caller.

Message Center: Another term for an answering service; it implies a sophistication and professionalism not associated with the stereotypical telephone answering service. Many telephone answering services use this term or one similar to distance themselves from these negative and atypical connotations.

Messaging: The act of answering a call, taking a message, processing that message, and relaying it to the client.

Operator: In this context, a generic term for one employed by a telephone answering service to answer calls, take messages, and distribute those messages (see, "TSR"). Often a more descriptive and positive term is used to avoid old-fashioned stereotypes. The label of Telephone Service Representative is preferred. Terms such as Telephone Secretary or Tele-Receptionist are also common. In other contexts, an Operator can refer to a Telephone Company Operator.

OPX (Off-premise extension): Just as one might have multiple extensions of their phone line in their house, this is a phone line extension at another location. Calls can be placed or answered at either location. Although not used too much anymore, OPX service was once used extensively to allow answering services to connect to and answer their client's lines. Because of lower cost and increased flexibility, call-forwarding has replaced OPX as the method of choice.

Order-taking (order entry): A large segment of inbound telemarketing whereby orders for products can be placed over the phone.

Outbound telemarketing: One of two aspects of telemarketing whereby a company proactively calls consumers or businesses in order to make sales. See, "inbound telemarketing."

Outsourcing: The concept of taking internal company functions and paying an outside firm to handle them instead. Outsourcing is done to save money, improve quality, and/or free company resources for other activities. Outsourcing was first done in the data-processing industry and has spread to areas, including telephone answering service, call centers, and telemarketing.

Paging: One of several dispatch methods used by telephone answering services. A pager is a small, specialized radio receiver which will alert the user when a message is received for the subscriber. There are four types of paging types: tone alert, voice, numeric display, and alphanumeric display, with the latter being the fastest growing type and numeric display being the most widely used.

Paperless: There are two general methods of providing telephone answering service. The traditional method is where messages are written on paper and is called "paper based." This method is obsolete and is only used by small or unsophisticated services. The other method is "paperless," meaning that no paper messages are involved, as all messages are typed into a computer. Once in the computer, they can be easily accessed, sorted, archived, faxed, or emailed. Most new equipment sales to the TAS industry are paperless systems.

PRI-ISDN (Primary-rate interface ISDN): A high-capacity version of ISDN which allows for twenty-three main channels (for voice, fax, or data) and one data channel (primarily for control purposes). See, "ISDN."

Queue: A "stack" of calls on hold (or ringing) and waiting to be answered. Many telephone answering services and most inbound call centers make use of a queue for increased efficiency, greater productivity, and overall shorter waiting times for callers.

Rep. (Representative): Another name for TSR.

Reseller: A long distance provider which does not own its own phone lines, but rather buys lines and/or time from another carrier at wholesale prices, to be resold at retail prices to the end user.

Reservation lines: A segment of inbound telemarketing whereby reservations and appointments can be scheduled over the phone.

Screen pop: In CTI (Computer-Telephony Integration) applications, causing a computer to display information about the call at the same time as the TSR answers the call. See, "CTI."

Skills-based routing: Skills based routing allows the call to be directed to the most available person who is knowledgeable and trained to handle the needs of the caller. The methodologies used to determine how the call will be routed can include database searches, DNIS, ANI, and DTMF notification (from an automated attendant) (St. Ledger, 1997, pp. 1-2).

TAS: An acronym for telephone answering service.

Telemarketing: Sales and marketing conducted using the telephone. It is classified as inbound or outbound. See, "inbound telemarketing" and "outbound telemarketing."

Telemessaging: A newer term to describe the activities performed by a telephone answering service. Some have attempted to recast the telephone answering service industry as the telemessaging industry to reflect a modern and more sophisticated approach and to distance themselves from the negative stereotypes of traditional telephone answering services.

Telephone Answering Service (Answering Service): A service whereby a client's phone is answered, a message is taken or information provided to the caller, and the results documented and dispatched to the client. The phones are answered in a central location. This is accomplished primarily by two methods: Having an extension of the client's phone connected to the office or by call-forwarding the client's line to the telephone answering service when it is to be answered.

Telephony: A term used to refer to telephone lines, trunks, circuits, related equipment, and the information (voice, fax, data, etc.) that is transmitted over them.

Teleweb: The interaction of web sites with call center at the click of a mouse button (Cooperstein, 1997, p. 37).

TSR (Telephone Service Representative): A term commonly used in the telemarketing and call center industries which is closely related to the telephone answering service industry. Other terms include, "agent," "rep.," and "operator."

Trunk: A telephone communications path between two points. One point is generally the telephone company's central office and the other being a secondary switch (Newton, 1989, p. 581).

Virtual Corporation: A small (usually one-person) company, which through the use of partnering and outsourcing can appear to be much larger than it actually is. Virtual companies have low overheard and low fixed costs, allowing them to be very flexible in meeting the needs of their customers.

Voice Mail: A general term to describe any method of electronically answering a telephone line, playing a prerecorded, digitized message, and possibly allowing the caller to leave a message and/or interact with it using touch tones. Types of voice mail systems include, call answering, announcement only, automated attendant, and IVR (interactive voice response.) Voice mail is not an answering machine, although it can function like one. Voice mail is a special computer which records all audio in a digital format, storing it on a hard disk drive, as opposed to magnetic tape as is done on some answering machines.

APPENDIX C: AUTHOR'S CONNECTION TO THIS RESEARCH

The author of this thesis and the researcher of the information contained therein is also the President of the Company. The author has been in the communications industry since 1979, which is essentially his entire adult working life. The majority of this time has been spent with the Company and the Company's predecessors. The author also worked for three years for an equipment manufacturer serving the telephone answering service industry. In addition, the author has served on various industry group boards and committees, has spoken at trade conventions and seminars, and has written for several industry publications.

APPENDIX D: EMAIL SOLICITATION FOR SURVEY PARTICIPATION

Subject: Your feedback is requested

Date: Thu, 23 Oct 1997 07:11:10 -0400

From: Peter L. DeHaan

To: ATSI Mailing List, NAEO, PI user group

Hi,

I am currently writing my master's thesis which is about the future of our industry. For part of my research, I would gratefully appreciate your input.

If you would be interested in answering a 5-question questionnaire, please let me know by emailing me directly at: dehaan@xxxxxxx.net

For those participants who are interested in the results of the research, I will make available a confidential and generic summary (that is all identities will be protected).

(This message is being posted to three mail lists; I apologize if you got it multiple times.)

Thank you for your assistance.

--

Peter DeHaan, President

Appendix E: Email Survey

Subject: Survey

Date: Fri, 24 Oct 1997 10:35:55 -0400

From: Peter L. DeHaan

To: [insert participant's email address]

[insert name]:

Thank you very much for your willingness to assist with my thesis research.

Instructions:

- Please read the definitions at the end of this message,

- click on "reply," and

- answer the following five questions, along with the profile which follows.

1) In general, what do you think are the strengths of bureaus in the TAS industry?

2) In general, what do you think are the weaknesses of bureaus in the TAS industry?

3) What do you think are the current opportunities for bureaus in the TAS industry?

4) What do you think are current threats to bureaus in the TAS industry?

5) In light of your answers, what would you recommend a bureau in the TAS industry do to prepare for the future?

Profile information

Your title:

Number of years in the TAS industry:

Your age group:

under 18

18 to 24

25 to 32

33 to 51

52 to 65

66 and above

Do you want to receive a summary of the results of this survey?

Your willingness to answer this questionnaire and assist with this research is greatly appreciated. Again, thank you.

[Definitions:

A Strength is a resource, skill, or other advantage relative to competitive alternatives.

A Weakness is a limitation or deficiency in resources, skills, or capabilities that seriously impedes an industry's effective performance.

An Opportunity is a major favorable situation in an industry's environment.

A Threat is a major unfavorable situation in an industry's environment.]

Appendix F: Second Request for Survey Completion

Subject: Survey

Date: Mon, 15 Dec 1997 09:22:20 -0500

From: Peter L. DeHaan

To: [insert participant's email address]

A few weeks ago, you expressed interest in completing a survey about the TAS industry for my master's thesis. To date, I have not received your completed survey. I need your feedback to make sure the results are valid. Here is another copy of the survey; I will need it returned to me by Saturday, December 20th, 8 a.m. EST to be included and for you to receive a summary of the results. Thank you.

Instructions:

- Please read the definitions at the end of this message,

- click on "reply," and

- answer the following five questions, along with the profile which follows.

1) In general, what do you think are the strengths of bureaus in the TAS industry?

2) In general, what do you think are the weaknesses of bureaus in the TAS industry?

3) What do you think are the current opportunities for bureaus in the TAS industry?

4) What do you think are current threats to bureaus in the TAS industry?

5) In light of your answers, what would you recommend a bureau in the TAS industry do to prepare for the future?

Profile information

Your title:

Number of years in the TAS industry:

Your age group:

under 18

18 to 24

25 to 32

33 to 51

52 to 65

66 and above

Do you want to receive a summary of the results of this survey?

Your willingness to answer this questionnaire and assist with this research is greatly appreciated. Again, thank you.

[Definitions:

A Strength is a resource, skill, or other advantage relative to competitive alternatives.

A Weakness is a limitation or deficiency in resources, skills, or capabilities that seriously impedes an industry's effective performance.

An Opportunity is a major favorable situation in an industry's environment.

A Threat is a major unfavorable situation in an industry's environment.]

APPENDIX G: NUMBER OF INDIVIDUALS CONTACTED FOR SURVEY PARTICIPATION

Table 20: <u>Number of Names on email Lists</u>

List Name	Total Names	Unique Names
ATSI	146	142
NAEO	57	56
<u>PIN</u>	<u>69</u>	<u>69</u>
Totals	272	267

Table 21: Email List Names Appearing on Multiple Lists

List Combination	Number Duplicated	Number of Representations
ATSI/NAEO	11	22
ATSI/PI	12	24
NAEO/PI	1	2
ATSI/NAEO/PI	1	3
Totals	25	51

Total unique names on each list:	267
Subtract "number of representations":	51
Add "number of duplicated names:"	25
Total unique names on all lists:	241

Figure 20: Analysis of the Number of Unique Email Names.

APPENDIX H: DETAILS OF INDUSTRY STRENGTHS

Table 12, in chapter 4, contained a summary of items listed as strength for the TAS industry. The table is repeated here for reference. The following, in Figure 21, is a breakdown of items comprising the category of "other" strengths. Each item received one mention on one survey, thereby representing four percent of the participants and approximately one percent of all responses. Although a minority viewpoint, these answers may have value and be worth considering because of their unique perspective.

- Ability to interface with client's equipment.

- Ability to meet outsourcing needs.

- Ability to deal with change.

- Acceptable profitability

- Customer loyalty

- Decreasing number of bureaus [that is, competitors]

- Employment opportunities for many people

- Low overhead

- Reporting capabilities

- Serve a niche market.

- Strong local connections

Figure 21: "Other" Industry Opportunities.

Table 12: <u>Summary of Opportunities</u> (repeated from chapter 4)

Category	Number of Answers	Percent of Participants	Percent of Total Answers
Flexibility	14	50%	20%
Staff ("Live" service)	13	46%	19%
Technology	11	39%	16%
Customer Focused	7	25%	10%
24 x 7	5	18%	7%
Established business	3	11%	4%
Multiple niches to serve	2	7%	3%
Solution oriented	2	7%	3%
Can manage entry-level staff	2	7%	3%
<u>Other</u>	<u>11</u>	<u>na</u>	<u>16%</u>
Totals	70	na	100%*

* Adjusted for rounding

APPENDIX I: DETAILS OF INDUSTRY WEAKNESSES

Table 13, in chapter 4, showed a summary of items listed as weaknesses for the TAS industry. The table is repeated here for reference. The following, in Figure 22, is a breakdown of items comprising the category of "other" weaknesses. Each item received one mention on one survey, thereby representing four percent of the participants and approximately one percent of all responses. Being a minority viewpoint, these answers may have value worth considering because of their unique perspective.

- Lack of diversity

- Capital intensive

- Price competition

- Subservient relationship to telephone companies

- Small, fragmented industry

- Can't standardize client solutions

Figure 22: "Other" Industry Weaknesses.

Table 13: <u>Summary of Weaknesses</u> (repeated from chapter 4)

Category	Number of Answers	Percent of Participants	Percent of Total Answers
Low rates	11	39%	14%
Poor management skills	10	36%	13%
Poor marketing ability	9	32%	11%
Poor service	8	29%	10%
Technology	6	21%	8%
Low pay (wages)	5	18%	6%
Bad image	5	18%	6%
Entry-level employees	5	18%	6%
Competition from technology	4	14%	5%
Under capitalization	4	14%	5%
Labor intensive	4	14%	5%
Inadequate training	2	7%	3%
<u>Other</u>	<u>6</u>	<u>na</u>	<u>8%</u>
Totals	70	na	100%*

* Adjusted for rounding

APPENDIX J: DETAILS OF INDUSTRY OPPORTUNITIES

Table 14, in chapter 4, showed a summary of items listed as opportunities for the TAS industry. The table is repeated here for reference. The following, in Figure 23, is a breakdown of items comprising the category of "other" opportunities. Each item received one mention on one survey, thereby representing approximately one percent of all responses. Being a minority viewpoint, these answers may have value worth considering because of their unique perspective. Note that some answers were ambiguous to the author and are quoted here as submitted.

- Aggressive pricing

- Aggressive service

- Selling ancillary services

- Appointment taking

- Back-lash to voice mail

- Diversification into related services

- Health care

- Increasingly mobile society

- Information gathering

- Large telecommunication companies' promotion of services

- Local peripheral services to become part of a nationwide networked facility

- Local, long distance, and calling cards

- Multi-tiered service offerings to large clients

- The need for twenty-four-hour coverage

- Proactive approach with telephone companies

- Provide niche call center services for call centers

- Steady revenue stream has improved perception among banks

- Strategic alliances with other bureaus

- Teleconferencing

- Telesales

Figure 23: "Other" Industry Opportunities.

Table 14: <u>Summary of Opportunities</u> (repeated from chapter 4)

Category	Number of Answers	Percent of Participants
Technology	13	15%
Telephone order-taking	9	11%
Internet	6	7%
Niche markets	6	7%
One-stop shopping	5	6%
Geographic expansion	4	5%
Help desk service	4	5%
Consolidation	3	4%
Customer service lines	3	4%
Marketing	2	2%
Enhanced services	2	2%
Outsourcing	2	2%
Overflow calls	2	2%
Integration with voice mail	2	2%
"Live" service	2	2%
<u>Other</u>	<u>20</u>	<u>24%</u>
Totals	85	100%*

* Adjusted for rounding

APPENDIX K: DETAILS OF INDUSTRY THREATS

Table 17, in chapter 4, showed a summary of items listed as threats to the TAS industry. The table is repeated here for reference. The following, in Figure 24, is a breakdown of items comprising the category of "other" threats. Each item received one mention on one survey, thereby representing approximately one percent of all responses. Being a minority viewpoint, these answers may have value worth considering because of their unique perspective. Note that some answers are in fact weaknesses and not threats. (See Appendix L for a breakdown).

- Depersonalized service as a result of acquisitions

- Lack of cooperation from the telephone company

- The telephone company providing service at no/low cost

- Low barrier to entry

- New entrants into the industry without historical bad habits

- Possible business cycle reversal

- Service being viewed as a commodity

- Our vendors selling equipment to our clients

- Family-owned services in a state of transition

- Lack of advertising effectiveness

- Service degradation resulting from consolidation

- Lack of size [economies of scale]

- Substitution of technology for people

Figure 24: "Other" Industry Threats.

Table 17: <u>Summary of Threats</u> (repeated from chapter 4)

Category	Number of Answers	Percent of Participants
Competitive forces	11	15%
Labor pressures	8	11%
Automation	5	7%
Technology	5	7%
Unprofessional	5	7%
Complacent	4	5%
Call centers	3	4%
Negative public perception	3	4%
Undercapitalization	3	4%
Low pricing	3	4%
Weak management	3	4%
Other answering services	2	3%
Bad debt	2	3%
Decreased demand for service	2	3%
Lack of vision for the future	2	3%
<u>Other</u>	<u>13</u>	<u>17%</u>
Totals	24	100%*

* Adjusted for rounding

Appendix L: Reclassification of Threats

As mentioned in Chapter 4, many of the items sited by participants as threats were in actuality, industry weaknesses. In fact, twenty-five of the seventy-four responses, or thirty-nine percent, were in fact weaknesses. (A weakness is an internal industry problem, whereas a threat is an external environmental issue.) Although all responses were included in the reporting and analysis of threats, it may prove useful to consider them properly divided into their respective categories of threats and weaknesses. As such, Table 22 lists only the true threats, whereas Table 23 lists those submitted as threats, which are actually weaknesses.

There are many similarities between the items listed in Table 23 ("Weaknesses Labeled as Threats by Participants) and Table 13 (Summary of Weaknesses). It will be left for the reader to make comparisons if so inclined. However, this would require making assumptions about the intent of the survey participants, an assumption the author is not prepared to make. Also refer to the complete list of weaknesses found in Appendix I.

Table 22: **True Threats**

Category	Number of Answers	Percent of Participants
Competitive forces	11	15%
Labor pressures	8	11%
Automation	5	7%
Technology	5	7%
Call centers	3	4%
Negative public perception	3	4%
Other answering services	2	3%
Bad debt	2	3%
Decreased demand for service	2	3%
Depersonalized service from acquisitions	1	1%
Lack of cooperation from telephone company	1	1%
Telephone company providing service at low cost	1	1%
Low barrier to entry	1	1%
New entrants without historical bad habits	1	1%
Possible business cycle reversal	1	1%
Service being viewed as a commodity	1	1%
Our vendors selling equipment to our clients	1	1%
Totals	49	61%

Table 23: <u>Weaknesses Labeled as Threats by Participants</u>

Category	Number of Answers	Percent of Participants
Unprofessional	5	7%
Complacent	4	5%
Undercapitalization	3	4%
Low pricing	3	4%
Weak management	3	4%
Lack of vision for the future	2	3%
Family-owned services in a state of transition	1	1%
Lack of advertising effectiveness	1	1%
Service degradation resulting from consolidation	1	1%
Lack of size [economies of scale]	1	1%
<u>Substitution of technology for people</u>	<u>1</u>	<u>1%</u>
Totals	25	39%

Appendix M: Detail of Recommended Options

Table 18, in chapter 4. showed a summary of recommendations for the TAS industry. The table is repeated here for reference. The following, in Figure 25, is a breakdown of items comprising the category of "other" recommendations. Each item received one mention on one survey, thereby representing approximately one percent of all responses. Being a minority viewpoint, these answers may have value worth considering because of their unique perspective.

- Develop teams.

- Do not dissipate your resources.

- Establish banking relationships.

- Establish financial controls.

- Get access to capital.

- Improve traditional weaknesses.

- Look at profitability necessary to fund growth.

- Make career paths for employees.

- Make decisions quickly.

- Network with multiple sites.

- Process internet orders.

- Provide one stop shopping.

- Stay away from being all things to all people.

Figure 25: "Other" Recommendations.

Table 18: Summary of Recommendations (repeated from chapter 4)

Category	Number of Answers	Percent of Participants
Acquire and use technology	16	17%
Improve staffing	13	14%
Increase knowledge	7	7%
Pursue niche markets	7	7%
Provide superior customer service	7	7%
Diversify	7	7%
Increase profitability	7	7%
Grow middle management	5	5%
Achieve economies of scale via acquisitions	3	3%
Improve public relations	3	3%
Invest in marketing	3	3%
Develop a vision for the future	3	3%
Combine personalized service with technology	2	2%
Other	13	14%
Totals	24	100% *

* Adjusted for rounding

APPENDIX N: KEY ALTERNATIVES

1. Growth via acquisition to achieve economies of scale.

- Viable and sound option

- Requires financing

- Will fail if not managed properly

2. Position business to be acquired.

- Excellent exit strategy

- Demand for well run, profitable operations will push prices up

3. Develop a market niche.

- What are the future prospects of the niche?

- How big is the niche?

- How much knowledge does the business possess on the niche?

4. Diversify into the call center industry.

- Already have relevant experience in staffing

- Requires greater space

- Necessitates an investment in equipment

5. Increase rates.

- Seemingly self-evident alternative

- Contrary to a "low-cost" provider paradigm

- A necessary requisite for many of the other options

6. Go public.

- Very high financial rewards for a successful initial public offering

- Loss of privacy and control

- Recommendation is to have ten million in annual revenue first

- May be a good long term goal

7. Improve sales and marketing efforts.

- Seemingly self-evident and necessary

- Another vehicle to finance other alternatives

8. Diversify into related industries.

- A hedge against a downturn in any single industry

- Could dilute financial and managerial resources too much

- Could stray too far from core competencies

9. Pursue internet opportunities.

- Email is projected to have a fifty percent penetration by 2001

- Will internet automation defeat the benefit of a "live" staff?

10. Develop a formal strategic plan.

- "Failing to plan is planning to fail"

- Industry entrepreneurs (as all entrepreneurs) plan as they go.

11. Perform a SWOT analysis.

- Will provide invaluable information

- Will form the basis for much of the strategic plan

- One more thing for management to do and spend time on

12. Acquire and use technology.

- Without an investment in technology, more staffing is needed

- Most regions have a shortage of qualified labor

- How much technology is enough?

- How will the investment in technology be financed?

13. Capitalize on 24-hour staffing.

- Make 24 x 7 staffing an asset

- Retain labor intensive condition as a barrier to entry

- The alternative is to eliminate staff using technology

14. Diversify into order-taking.

- Order-taking is a good, first step into the call center industry.

- All staffing issues (hiring, training, scheduling) are more intense

- Space requirements are likely greater

- Client expectations are higher

Figure 26: <u>Overview of Analysis of Key Alternatives.</u>

BIBLIOGRAPHY

ACETS. (1997, Oct 20). [Internet, http://www.acets.com/index/service/]

BCSI (Business Communications Services International). (1997, Nov 25). [Internet, http://www.bcsi.org/]

Berkowitz E., Kerin R., Hartley S., & Rudelius W. (1997). Marketing (5th ed.). Chicago: Irwin.

Blowers S., Ericksen G. & Milan T. (1995). The Ernst & Young guide to taking your company public. New York: John Riley Sons, Inc.

Carter, M. (1997, Dec 3). Things are changing in the TAS industry. [http://www.connectionsmagazine.com/docs/page45.html], pp. 1-4.

Christiansen, L. (1997, June 29). Call center industry struggles to find new hires. The Oakland Tribune, pp. D-1, D-3.

Church, B. (1995, May). Call center consolidation: Questions to ask, pitfalls to avoid. Service Level Newsletter, pp. 8-9.

Collins, J. (1997, Oct). What comes next? Inc., 41-50.

Connection magazine adds alarm companies: Subscription base now 39,000! (1997, May/Jun). Connections Magazine, p. 41.

Cooperestein, D. (1997, Oct 1). Click here for an agent. <u>CIO</u>, pp. 36, 38, 39.

Davis S. & Davidson B. (1991). <u>2020 Vision</u>. New York: Simon & Schuster.

Don't sell yourself short. (1996, Winter). <u>The Communicator</u>, pp. 5, 7.

<u>Economic impact: US direct marketing today</u>. (1997, Oct 20). [Internet, http:// www.the-dma.org]

Emmet, R. (1997a, Sep/Oct). Future trends: We have special business solutions unavailable from any other communications companies. <u>Connections Magazine</u>, pp. 16, 22, 41.

Emmet, R. (1997b, Oct 20). <u>What will the new communications service bureau of the late 90s be like</u>? [Internet, http://www.tasmarketing. com/docs/future.htm]

Fenn, D. (1997, Nov). No more business as usual. <u>Inc.</u>, pp. 114, 119.

Hastings, M. (1996, Summer). The rest of the iceberg. <u>Answer</u>, pp. 11-13.

Knowledge is power in selling and buying a business. (1997, Sep/Oct). <u>Connections Magazine</u>, 6-7. (Reprinted from Business Opportunity Journal, 1997, July).

Kuhn, M. (1995, Mar/Apr). Where are we coming from? Where are we going? <u>Answer</u>, pp. 12–17.

<u>Making the most of an effective medium: DMA's guidelines for marketing by telephone</u>. (1997, Oct 20). [Internet, http://www.the-dma.org]

Michaels, C. (1997a, Mar/Apr). Designing the telecommunications center of the future: Part I. [http://www.connectionsmagazine.com/docs]

Michaels, C. (1997b, May/Jun). Designing the telecommunications center of the future: Part II. Connections Magazine, pp. 12, 46-47.

Michaels, S. (1997a, Sep/Oct). If you are thinking about selling ... now is the time. Connections Magazine, back cover.

Michaels, S. (1997b, Oct 20). How not to sell your telephone answering service. [Internet, http://www.tasmarketing.com/docs/hownot.htm]

Michaels, S. (1997c, Oct 20). How to start an answering service. [Internet, http://www.tasmarketing.com/docs/howto.htm]

Mintzberg, H. & Quinn, J. (1991) The strategy process (2nd ed.). Englewood Cliffs, NJ: Prentice Hall, Inc.

Morrison, I. (1996, No. 2). [Review of The second curve: Managing the velocity of change]. Inc., p.18.

Murray, T. (1997a, Jul/Aug) Call centers: Enhanced telephone services. [http://www.connectionsmagazine.com/docs/page8.html], pp. 1-8.

Murray, T. (1997b, Jul/Aug) The role of the owner. Connections Magazine, pp. 18, 26.

Naisbitt, J. & Aburdene P. (1990). Megatrends 2000. New York: William Morrow and company.

Nash, J. (1997, Oct 1). Fast fone farms, fat profits. CIO, pp. 40-52.

Newton, H. (1989). Newton's telecom dictionary: The official Glossary of Telecommunications acronyms, terms and jargon (2nd ed.). New York: Telecom Library.

Orsino P. (1994). Successful business expansion. New York: John Riley and Sons, Inc.

Osmon, M. (1997, Oct 30). From TAS to call center: Making the big move. [Internet, http:/www.atsi.org/icenter/move.html]

Page, J. (1997, Oct 20). Paging and the TAS industry: An opportunity for synergy. [Internet, http://www.atsi.org/icenter/paging.html]

Pearce J. & Robinson R. (1997). Strategic management: Formulation, implementation, and control (6th ed.). Chicago: Richard D. Irwin, a Times Mirror Higher Education Group, Inc. company.

Shatz, O. (1996, Winter). TAS is back! The Communicator, pp. 12, 14.

Smith, T. (1996, Spring). How to surf a billion-dollar wave. Answer, p. 9.

St. Ledger, B. (1997, Oct 26). Solving customer care and marketing problems with call center technology. [Internet, http://www. telecoms-magazine/articles/jul97/ledger.html]

TAS history. 1989). Answer, pp. 30-34.

Taylor, B. (1995, Winter). Discovering 'new ways to dream.' Answer, pp. 16-17.

Whitford, D. (1996, Spring) The Marketeer. Answer, 17-20.

www.ingramcontent.com/pod-product-compliance
Lightning Source LLC
Chambersburg PA
CBHW062129020426

42335CB00013B/1156